KETO DIET COOKBOOK

2 Books in 1: Most Effective Keto Diet Cookbook for Weight Control with 40+ Delicious and Effortless Keto Bread and Chaffles Recipes in this Keto Diet Cookbook for Beginners for People of any Age.

KETO BREAD COOKBOOK

KETO CHAFFLESS RECIPES

KETO BREAD COOKBOOK

Table of content

INTRODUCTION

If I were stuck on a desert island, I know exactly what my choice for survival food would be: bread and butter. Biscuits, muffins, cinnamon buns, yeast bread —I like them all. I have been baking bread since I was a teenager, and today it is still a pleasure to turn a few simple ingredients into a colossal popover or see a buttermilk loaf rise high in the oven and then eat it.

All the bread I bake takes only a short time to put together, and then I fit finishing them—usually shaping and baking them—around my schedule. I assemble scones, cornbread, crusty loaves, and doughnuts in minutes. I make yeast-leavened sticky buns, brioche, dark rye, and a crusty multigrain loaf that sit in the refrigerator for as long as several days. They wait to be baked until I have the time or the inclination, and then they rise just once in the pan. My buttery rolls, cheese loaves, buttermilk loaf, focaccia, and nut-and-fruit whole-wheat rounds are all batter bread made from soft yeast dough. They are mixed with an electric mixer, in a food processor, or by hand, and rise just once in the pan immediately after mixing and shaping. Morning toast and crumpets, lunchtime sandwiches, and dinner rolls— bread is an important part of every meal. Good bread is a given; nurturing, pride, and enjoyment are your gifts.

Years ago, David Gayson, the late American essayist and journalist, aptly wrote, "Talk of joy: there may be things better than beef stew and baked potatoes and homemade bread—there may be.

RECIPES

1. BUTTER DROP BISCUITS

YIELD: Makes six biscuits| **MIXING TIME**: 5 minutes |**BAKING**: 475°F for about 12 minutes

INGREDIENTS

- 6 tbsp unsalted butter
- ½ cups unbleached all-purpose flour
- ¼ cup cake flour
- 1 tbsp granulated sugar
- 2 tsp baking powder
- 1 tsp baking soda
- 1 tsp kosher salt
- ¼ cup cold shortening, cut into pieces
- 1 cup cold buttermilk, any fat content

METHOD

1. Preheat oven to 475°F.

2. In a heavy, 9-in ovenproof frying pan, melt the butter over low heat. Set aside.

3. Sift both flour, sugar, baking powder, baking soda, and salt into a large bowl. Scatter the shortening over the top. Using your thumb and fingertips, two table knives, or a pastry blender, work the shortening into the flour mixture until flour-coated pea-sized pieces form. There will still be some loose flour. Make a well in the center, pour the buttermilk into the well, and use a large spoon to mix the buttermilk into the dry ingredients to form a soft dough.

4. Using a ¼-cup capacity ice cream scoop or the large spoon, drop six rounded scoops of dough into the prepared pan, spacing them about ½ in apart (drop 5

5. Biscuits in a circle around the edge of the pan and one biscuit in the middle). Using the large spoon, carefully turn over each biscuit to coat both sides with butter.

6. Bake until the tops are golden, about 12 minutes. Serve warm, directly from the pan.

7. The biscuits can be baked up to 3 hours ahead and left in the pan, covered loosely with aluminum foil. To serve, preheat the oven to 275°F and reheat the covered biscuits until warm, about 10 minutes.

2. VERY BIG POPOVERS

YIELD: Makes six popovers |MIXING TIME: 5 minutes |REFRIGERATOR TIME: 20 minutes to 2 hours |BAKING:425°F for about 45 minutes, plus 10 minutes' resting time in the oven

INGREDIENTS

- Flavorless nonstick cooking spray for muffin wells
- three large eggs
- 1½ cups milk, any fat content
- ¾ tsp kosher salt
- 1½ cups unbleached all-purpose flour
- Butter and jam or Blueberry Sauce

METHOD

1. Have ready a rimmed baking sheet. Generously spray six wells in a jumbo muffin tin with flavorless nonstick cooking spray.

2. Whisk the eggs, milk, and salt until blended. Slowly whisk in the flour just until incorporated. The batter will have small lumps of flour but no large globs. Tap the whisk lightly on the side of the bowl if the flour clumps in the wires. Refrigerate the batter for 20 minutes or up to 2 hours.

3. The prepared muffin tin on the baking sheet. Using a scant ½ cup batter for each popover, pour the batter into the prepared wells. The batter should be at least ¼ in from the rim of each well.

4. Turn on the oven to 425°F. Bake until the tops and exposed edges are browned, about 45 minutes. The popovers will rise high over the tops of the cups. Turn off the oven. Using a toothpick, puncture the risen sides in each popover in three places, and let the popovers sit in the turned-off oven with the oven door closed for 10 minutes. This releases some of

the steam in the popovers.

5. Remove as many popovers as needed for a first serving, and leave the remaining ones in the oven for up to 30 minutes to keep warm. Serve with butter and jam.

3. SAVORY LEMON-LEEK LOAF

YIELD: Makes one loaf |**MIXING TIME**: 10 minutes |**BAKING 375°F for about 50 minutes**

INGREDIENTS

- 1 tbsp butter
- 2 cups leeks
- 2 cups unbleached all-purpose flour
- ½ tsp baking soda
- ½ tsp baking powder
- ½ tsp kosher salt
- four large eggs
- 1½ cups sour cream
- 1 tbsp grated lemon zest
- ½ tsp freshly ground black pepper

METHOD

1. Preheat to 375°F. Butter a 9-by-5-by-3-in loaf pan (or any loaf pan with an 8-cup capacity). Line the pan with parchment and butter the paper.
2. In a frying pan over medium heat, melt the butter. Add the leeks and cook, often stirring, until softened, about 5 minutes. Remove from the heat.
3. In a bowl, stir the flour, baking soda, baking powder, and salt. Set aside.
4. Whisk the eggs until blended. Using a large spoon, stir in the sour cream, leeks with any pan liquid, lemon zest, and pepper. Add the flour mixture and stir until blended and a sticky dough forms. Scrape the dough into the prepared pan.
5. Bake until the top feels firm and is golden brown, about 50 minutes. Let cool for about 15 minutes.

4. TOASTED PECAN&

CHOCOLATE CHUNK SCONES

YIELD Makes eight scones |MIXING TIME 10 minutes |BAKING: 400°F for about 18 minutes

INGREDIENTS

- 2 cups unbleached all-purpose flour
- ¼ cup granulated sugar
- 1¼ tsp baking powder
- ¼ tsp baking soda
- ¼ tsp kosher salt
- ½ cup cold unsalted butter,
- cup buttermilk, any fat content
- 2 tbsp pure maple syrup
- 3 oz. semisweet chocolate, chopped
- ½ cup pecans, toasted and coarsely chopped

- one large egg beat with 1 tbsp heavy cream for egg wash·

METHOD

1. Preheat oven t to 400°F. Line a baking sheet with parchment paper.
2. In a bowl, whisk the flour, sugar, baking powder, baking soda, and salt. Scatter the butter pieces over the top. Using your thumb and fingertips, two table knives, or a pastry blender, work the butter into the flour mixture until flour-coated pea-sized pieces form. There will still be some loose flour. Pour the buttermilk and maple syrup into the center, and use a large spoon to mix them into the dry ingredients to form soft dough. Stir in the chocolate and pecans.
3. With floured hands, gather up the dough and put it on a lightly floured work surface. Knead the dough about five strokes
4. Cut the circle into eight wedges by cutting it into quarters and then cutting the quarters in half. Use a wide spatula to transfer the scones to the prepared baking sheet, spacing them

about 1½ in apart.

5. Bake until the tops are lightly browned, and the bottoms are browned for about 18 minutes. Transfer to cool for at least 15 minutes before serving. Accompany with whipped cream, if desired.

6. The scones can be baked one day ahead, covered, and stored at room temperature. To serve, preheat the oven to 275°F and reheat the scones until warm, about 15 minutes.

5. CHERRY & ALMOND WHOLE-WHEAT SCONES

YIELD: Makes eight scones |**MIXING TIME**: 10 minutes |**BAKING**: 400°F for about 15 minutes

INGREDIENTS

- 1½ cups unbleached all-purpose flour
- ½ cup whole-wheat flour
- ½ cup granulated sugar, plus 2 tsp
- 1 tsp baking powder
- 1 tsp baking soda
- ½ tsp kosher salt
- 1 tsp ground cinnamon
- 1 tsp grated orange zest
- ½ cup cold butter,
- 1 tsp pure vanilla extract
- ½ tsp pure almond extract
- ¾ cup buttermilk, any fat content

- ½ cup dried pitted cherries
- one large egg, lightly beaten, for egg wash
- 3 tbsp natural or blanched sliced almonds or coarsely chopped natural almonds
- Cherry jam and butter or clotted cream for serving

METHOD

1. Preheat the oven to 400°F. Line a baking sheet with parchment paper.

2. In a bowl, whisk flours, the ½ cup sugar, the baking powder, baking soda, salt, and cinnamon. Stir in the orange zest. Scatter the butter pieces over the top. Using your thumb and fingertips, two table knives, or a pastry blender, work the butter into the flour mixture until flour-coated pea-sized pieces form. There will still be some loose flour. Make a well in the center, add the buttermilk, vanilla, almond extract, and cherries to the well, and use a large spoon to mix them into the dry ingredients to form a soft dough.

3. Gather the batter into a softball, put it on a floured rolling surface, and pat it into an 8-in

circle about ¾ in thick. Cut the circle into eight wedges.

4. Sprinkle the almonds evenly over the top, pressing them gently onto the dough. Sprinkle the remaining 2 tsp sugar over the nuts.

5. Bake until the tops are lightly colored, the edges are lightly browned, and the bottoms are browned for about 15 minutes. Let cool for at least 15 minutes before serving. Accompany with jam and butter.

6. The scones can be baked one day ahead, covered, and left at room temperature. To serve, preheat the oven to 275°F and reheat the scones until warm, about 15 minutes.

6. PUMPKIN-CHOCOLATE CHIP PANCAKES

YIELD: **It makes twelve 4-in pancakes |MIXING TIME**: **10 minutes |COOKING**: **4½ to 6 minutes per batch**

INGREDIENTS

- 1 cup unbleached all-purpose flour
- 1 tsp baking powder
- ½ tsp baking soda
- ¼ tsp kosher salt
- 1 tsp. ground cinnamon
- ½ tsp. ground ginger
- ¾ cup milk, any fat content
- one large egg
- 3 tbsp. pure maple syrup
- ¾ cup canned pumpkin

- ¼ cup full-fat or low-fat plain yogurt
- cup semisweet chocolate chips
- 2 tbsp. unsalted butter
- 1 cup vanilla yogurt for serving

METHOD

1. Sift the baking powder, flour, baking soda, salt, cinnamon, and ginger into a medium bowl. Add the milk, egg, maple syrup, pumpkin, and plain yogurt. Stir the batter until blended, and there is no loose flour. You may see some small lumps; that's okay. Stir in the chocolate chips just until evenly distributed.

2. Preheat the oven to 250° F. You will be keeping the first batches of pancakes warm in the oven until all the batter is used.

3. Heat a pan, and add 1 tbsp. of the butter. Using a pastry brush (preferably silicone); spread the butter evenly over the surface. Using 3 tbsp. for each pancake, scoop the batter onto the hot griddle, being careful not to crowd the pancakes. After 3 to 4 minutes, when bubbles have formed near the pancakes' edges (they will not bubble in the center), the edges have begun to look dry, and the underside is golden

brown; carefully turn the pancakes with a spatula.

4. Transfer to a platter and place in the oven. Do not cover the pancakes or they will become get soggy. Repeat with the remaining batter, adding additional butter to the skillet as needed.

5. Serve the pancakes hot and pass the vanilla yogurt at the table.

7. CHRISTMAS MORNING BELGIAN WAFFLES

YIELD: It makes sixteen 4-in square waffles |**MIXING TIME**: 10 minutes |**COOKING**: About 3 minutes per batch

INGREDIENTS

- ·Flavorless nonstick cooking spray or corn or canola oil for the waffle iron
- 2 cups unbleached all-purpose flour
- 2½ tsp. baking powder
- ¾ tsp. baking soda
- ½ tsp. salt
- four large eggs, separated
- 1½ cups whole milk
- 1 cup full-fat or low-fat plain yogurt
- ½ cup unsalted butter, melted

- 2 tbsp. pure maple syrup
- Toppings of choice for serving

METHOD

1. Spray waffle iron with flavorless nonstick cooking spray or brush lightly with oil. Heat the waffle iron—Preheat the oven to 250°F. You will be keeping the cooked waffles warm in the oven until all the batter is used.

2. Sift together the flour, baking powder, baking soda, and salt into a medium bowl. In a large bowl, whisk together the egg yolks, milk, yogurt, melted butter, and maple syrup until blended. A few bits of melted butter may firm up; that's okay. In a spotlessly clean large bowl, using an electric mixer on medium-high speed, beat the egg whites until firm peaks form.

3. Stir the flour into the egg yolk just until combined. Using a rubber spatula, fold the egg whites into the batter until no white specks are visible.

4. Spoon enough batter evenly onto the hot waffle iron to fill it, according to the manufacturer's

directions. Cook it until the waffles are browned for about 3 minutes. The waffles are ready if you lift the waffle iron's top; the waffle releases easily from it. Also, the steam escaping from the seam of the iron will have subsided. Transfer to an ovenproof platter and keep warm in the oven. Repeat to cook the remaining batter.

5. Serve the waffles hot with one or more toppings of choice.

8. BACON & CHEDDAR CORNBREAD

YIELD : It makes one 9-in square loaf |MIXING TIME: 10 minutes |BAKING: 400°F for about 20 minutes

INGREDIENTS

- 1 cup unbleached all-purpose flour
- ¼ cup granulated sugar
- 2 tsp. baking powder
- 1 tsp. baking soda
- ½ tsp. kosher salt
- 1¼ cups fine-or medium-grind stoneground yellow cornmeal
- 1½ cups buttermilk, any fat content
- One large egg
- 2 tbsp. unsalted butter, melted
- Four thick slices of bacon (about 5 oz. total), fried crisp, drained and broken into small pieces
- 1 cup shredded Cheddar cheese

METHOD

1. Preheat the oven to 400°F.
2. Butter a 9-in square pan with 2-in sides.
3. Stir in the cornmeal and set aside. In a bowl, using a fork, stir together the buttermilk, egg, and melted butter until blended. Pour the flour
4. Mixture over the buttermilk mixture and use a spoon to stir the batter. Stir in the bacon and cheese. Scrape into the prepared pan.
5. Bake until the top feels firm if lightly touched and a toothpick inserted in the center comes out clean, about 20 minutes. Let cool in the pan, then cut into squares and serve warm.

9. BUTTERMILK CORNBREAD

YIELD: It makes one 8-in square bread. |**MIXING TIME**: 10 minutes |**BAKING**: 400°F for about 20 minutes

INGREDIENTS

- 1 tbsp. unsalted butter, plus 4 tbsp. melted butter
- 1 cup unbleached all-purpose flour
- 13 cup granulated sugar
- 2 tsp. baking powder
- 1 tsp. baking soda
- ½ tsp. kosher salt
- 1 cup fine-grind stoneground yellow cornmeal
- 1¼ cups buttermilk, any fat content
- One large egg

METHOD

1. Preheat the oven to 400°F. Put the 1 tbsp. butter in an 8-in square pan with 2-in sides.

2. Sift together the flour, sugar, baking powder, baking soda, and salt into a medium bowl. Stir in the cornmeal and set aside. In a bowl, stir together the buttermilk, egg, and the 4 tbsp. melted butter until blended. Pour the flour into the buttermilk mixture and stir the batter slowly.

3. Coat the pan with the melted butter. The butter may be browned (this is fine) but should not be burnt. Scrape the batter into the prepared pan.

4. Bake until the top feels firm if lightly touched and a toothpick inserted in the center comes out clean, about 20 minutes. Cut into squares and serve warm.

10. SOUTHERN CORN STICKS

YIELD: It makes seven corn sticks. |**MIXING TIME**: 10 minutes |**BAKING**: 425°F for about 15 minutes

INGREDIENTS

- 2 tbsp. unsalted butter, melted
- 1 tsp. corn or canola oil plus 1 tbsp.
- 2 tbsp. unbleached all-purpose flour
- ¾ cup fine-grind stoneground yellow cornmeal
- 1 tbsp. granulated sugar
- ½ tsp. baking powder
- ½ tsp. baking soda
- ¼ tsp. kosher salt
- ½ cup buttermilk, any fat content

- One large egg

METHOD

1. Preheat the oven to 425°F.
2. In a pan, melt the butter with 1 tsp. of oil. Use a pastry brush to brush the corn stick pan or butter-oil mixture. Heat the pan while you mix the batter.
3. In a bowl, stir together the flour, cornmeal, sugar, baking powder, baking soda, and salt. Add the buttermilk, egg, and 1 tbsp. oil and stir the batter slowly. The batter will fill to the rim.
4. Bake until the tops are browned. Do not want to turn the pan upside down to release the corn sticks because it could weigh them down and break them. Serve warm.

11. APRICOT CORN MUFFINS

YIELD: It makes six large muffins. |MIXING TIME: 10 minutes |BAKING: 375°F for about 20 minutes

INGREDIENTS

- 1 cup fine-grind stoneground yellow cornmeal
- 1 cup unbleached all-purpose flour
- 1 tsp. baking powder
- 1 tsp. baking soda
- ½ tsp. kosher salt
- ½ cup whole milk
- 6 tbsp. unsalted butter, melted
- 13 cup pure maple syrup
- Two large eggs
- ½ cup dried apricots, coarsely chopped

METHOD

1. Preheat the oven to 375°F.
2. Butter six wells (each with 1-cup capacity) in a jumbo muffin tin.
3. Stir together the cornmeal, flour, baking powder, baking soda, and salt. In a large bowl, stir the milk, butter, maple syrup, and eggs until blended. Stir in the apricot pieces. Pour the flour mixture over the milk mixture, and use a large spoon to stir the batter slowly. You will have 3 cups of batter. Pour ½ cup batter into each prepared muffin well.
4. Bake until the tops feel firm if lightly touched and are evenly browned (signaling the sides are browned), and a toothpick inserted in the center of a muffin comes out clean, about 20 minutes. Run a small, sharp knife around the inside edge of each well to loosen the muffin sides, then turn the muffins out onto the rack to cool for at least 15 minutes. Serve warm.

12. HUSH PUPPIES

YIELD: It takes about 20 fritters. |MIXING TIME : 10 minutes |FRYING: About 4 minutes per batch at 365°F.

INGREDIENTS

- 1 cup fine-or medium-grind stoneground yellow cornmeal
- ½ cup unbleached all-purpose flour
- 1½ tsp. baking soda
- ½ tsp. kosher salt
- 1 cup buttermilk, any fat content
- One large egg, lightly beaten
- One medium yellow onion, finely chopped
- Corn oil for deep-frying
- Kosher or sea salt for finishing

METHOD

1. In a bowl, stir flour, baking soda, and salt. Stir in the buttermilk and egg just to moisten and blend the ingredients. Stir in the onion.

2. Line a baking sheet with paper towels and place it near the stove. Pour 2 in of oil into a heavy, medium saucepan and heat over medium heat to 365°F on a deep-frying thermometer. Using a large spoon, drop the batter by tablespoons into the hot oil, frying 6 or 7 at a time. The batter will puff and float to the top. Fry until the undersides are browned, about 2 minutes. Using a slotted spoon, turn and fry on the second side until a deep golden brown, about 2 minutes longer. Using the slotted spoon, transfer to the towel-lined pan to drain.

3. Fry the remaining batter the same way in two batches, allowing the oil to return to 365°F before adding each batch. Sprinkle lightly with salt and serve immediately.

13.ALMOND COCONUT MUFFINS

YIELD: Makes five muffins |MIXING TIME: 5 minutes |BAKING: 300°F for about 15minutes

INGREDIENTS

- 6 tbsp. unsalted butter
- ½ cups unbleached coconut flour
- ¼ cup almond flour
- 1 tbsp. granulated sugar
- 2 tsp. baking powder
- 1 tsp. baking soda
- 1 tsp. kosher salt
- ¼ cup cold shortening, cut into pieces
- 1 cup cold buttermilk, any fat content

METHOD

1. Preheat the oven to 475°F.

2. In a heavy, 9-in ovenproof frying pan, melt the butter over low heat. Set aside.

3. Sift both flour, sugar, baking powder, baking soda, and salt into a large bowl. Scatter the shortening over the top. Using your thumb and fingertips, two table knives, or a pastry blender, work the shortening into the flour mixture until flour-coated pea-sized pieces form. There will still be some loose flour. Pour the buttermilk and use a large spoon to mix the buttermilk into the dry ingredients to form soft dough.

4. Using a ¼-cup capacity ice cream scoop or the large spoon, drop six rounded scoops of dough into the prepared pan, spacing them about ½ in apart (drop 5 Muffins in a circle around the edge of the pan and one biscuit in the middle). Using the large spoon, carefully turn over each biscuit to coat both sides with butter.

5. Bake until the tops are golden, about 12 minutes. Serve warm, directly from the pan.

6. The muffins can be baked up to 3 hours ahead and left in the pan, covered loosely with aluminum foil.

14. BLUBERRY MUFFINS

YIELD: Makes six muffins |**MIXING TIME**: 5 minutes |**REFRIGERATOR TIME**: 10 minutes to 2 hours |**BAKING**: 425°F for about 45 minutes, plus 10 minutes' resting time in the oven

INGREDIENTS

- Flavorless nonstick cooking spray for muffin wells
- three large eggs
- 1½ cups milk, any fat content
- ¾ tsp. kosher salt
- 1½ cups unbleached all-purpose flour
- Butter and jam or Blueberry Sauce for serving

METHOD

1. Have ready a rimmed baking sheet. Generously spray six wells in a jumbo muffin tin (or use one of the alternative baking containers suggested in the introductory note) with flavorless nonstick cooking spray.

2. In a bowl, whisk the milk, eggs, and salt until blended. Slowly whisk in the flour just until incorporated. The batter will have small lumps of flour but no large globs. Tap the whisk lightly on the side of the bowl if the flour clumps in the wires.

3. The prepared muffin tin on the baking sheet. Using a scant ½ cup batter for each popover, pour the batter into the prepared wells. The batter should be at least ¼ in from the rim of each well.

4. Turn on the oven to 425°F. Bake until the tops and exposed edges are browned, about 45 minutes. The popovers will rise high over the tops of the cups. Turn off the oven. Using a toothpick, puncture the risen sides in each popover in three places, and let the popovers sit in the turned-off oven with the oven door

closed for 10 minutes. This releases some of the steam in the popovers.

5. Remove as many popovers as needed for a first serving, and leave the remaining ones in the oven for up to 30 minutes to keep warm. Serve with butter and jam.

15.CREAMY LEMON PANCAKES

YIELD: Makes one pancake |MIXING TIME: 10 minutes |BAKING: 375°F for about 50 minutes

INGREDIENTS

- 1 tbsp. unsalted butter
- 2 cups chopped leeks
- 2 cups unbleached all-purpose flour
- ½ tsp. baking soda
- ½ tsp. baking powder
- ½ tsp. kosher salt
- Four large eggs
- ½ cups sour cream
- 1 tbsp. grated lemon zest
- ½ tsp. freshly ground black pepper

METHOD

1. Preheat the oven to 375°F. Butter a 9-by-5-by-3-in loaf pan (or any loaf pan with an 8-cup capacity).

2. In a frying pan, melt the butter. Add the leeks and cook, often stirring, until softened, about 5 minutes. Remove from the heat.

3. In a medium bowl, stir together the flour, baking soda, baking powder, and salt. Set aside.

4. In a bowl, whisk the eggs. Using a large spoon, stir in the sour cream, leeks with any pan liquid, lemon zest, and pepper. Add the flour and stir, and a sticky dough forms. Scrape the dough into the prepared pan.

5. Bake until the top feels firm and is golden brown, about 50 minutes. Let cool completely before serving.

6. It is good toasted or cooked with a filling in a Panini grill.

16.TOASTED CHOCOBUTTER DELIGHT

YIELD: Makes six |MIXING TIME: 10 minutes

BAKING: 400°F for about 18 minutes

INGREDIENTS

- 2 cups unbleached all-purpose flour
- ¼ cup granulated sugar
- 1¼ tsp. baking powder
- ¼ tsp. baking soda
- ¼ tsp. kosher salt
- ½ cup cold butter,
- cup buttermilk, any fat content
- 2 tbsp. pure maple syrup
- 3 oz. semisweet chocolate, chopped
- ½ cup pecans, toasted and coarsely chopped
- one large egg

- 1 tbsp. heavy cream for egg wash
- Vanilla whipped cream for serving (optional

METHOD

1. Preheat the oven to 400°F. Line a baking sheet with parchment paper.
2. In a bowl, whisk the flour, sugar, baking soda, and salt. Scatter the butter pieces over the top. Using your thumb and fingertips, two table knives, or a pastry blender, work the butter into the flour mixture until flour-coated pea-sized pieces form. There will still be some loose flour. Pour the buttermilk and maple syrup into the well, and use a large spoon to mix them into the dry ingredients to form a soft dough. Stir in the chocolate and pecans.
3. With floured hands, gather up the dough and put it on a lightly floured work surface. Knead the dough about five strokes: push down and away with the heel of your hand against the surface, then fold the dough in half toward you, and rotate it a quarter turn, flouring the surface as necessary to prevent sticking. Lightly flour the work surface again and pat the dough into a

7-in circle 1¼ in thick. transfer the scones to the dish

4. Bake till browned, and the bottoms are browned for about 18 minutes. Transfer to a wire rack to cool for at least 15 minutes before serving. Accompany with whipped cream, if desired.

5. The scones can be baked one day ahead, covered, and stored.

17. VANILLA WHEAT SCONES

YIELD: Makes six scones |MIXING TIME: 15 mins |BAKING: 350°F for about 15 mins

INGREDIENTS

- ½ cup cold butter,
- 1 tsp. pure vanilla extract
- ½ tsp. pure almond extract
- ¾ cup buttermilk, any fat content
- ½ cup dried pitted cherries
- 1½ cups unbleached all-purpose flour
- ½ cup whole-wheat flour
- ½ cup granulated sugar, plus 2 tsp.
- 1 tsp. baking powder
- 1 tsp. baking soda
- ½ tsp. kosher salt
- 1 tsp. ground cinnamon
- 1 tsp. grated orange zest

- One egg
- 3 tbsp. natural or blanched sliced almonds or coarsely chopped natural almonds
- Cherry jam and butter or clotted cream for serving

METHOD

1. Preheat the oven to400°F. Line a baking sheet with parchment paper.

2. In a bowl, beat together both flours, the ½ cup sugar, the baking powder, baking soda, salt, and cinnamon. Stir in the orange zest. Scatter the butter pieces over the top. Using your thumb and fingertips, two table knives, or a pastry blender, work the butter into the flour mixture until flour-coated pea-sized pieces form. There will still be some loose flour. Make a well in the center, add the buttermilk, vanilla, almond extract, and cherries to the well, and mix them into the dry ingredients to form a soft dough.

3. Gather the dough into a softball, put it on a floured rolling surface, and pat it into an 8-in circle about ¾ in thick. Cut the circle into eight

wedges

4. By cutting it into quarters and then cutting the quarters in half. Use a wide spatula to transfer the scones to the prepared baking sheet, placing them about three apart. Brush the tops with the egg wash. . Sprinkle the almonds evenly over the top, pressing them gently onto the dough. Sprinkle the remaining 2 tsp. sugar over the nuts.

5. Bake until the tops are colored, the edges are browned, and the bottoms are browned for about 15 mins. Transfer to cool for at least 15 mins before serving. Accompany with jam and butter.

6. The scones can be baked one day ahead, covered.

18. HINTY GINGER PANCAKES

YIELD: Makes 4-in pancakes |**MIXING TIME: 10 mins** |**COOKING**: 4½ to 6 mins per batch

INGREDIENTS

- 3 tbsp. pure maple syrup
- ¾ cup canned pumpkin
- ¼ cup full-fat or low-fat plain yogurt
- cup semisweet chocolate chips
- 2 tbsp. unsalted butter
- 1 cup vanilla yogurt for serving
- 1 cup unbleached all-purpose flour
- 1 tsp. baking powder
- ½ tsp. baking soda
- ¼ tsp. kosher salt
- 1 tsp. ground cinnamon

- ½ tsp. ground ginger
- ¾ cup milk, any fat content
- One egg

METHOD

1. Sift the flour, salt, baking powder, cinnamon, and ginger into a bowl. Add the milk, egg, maple syrup, pumpkin, and plain yogurt. Using a spoon, stir the batter until all the ingredients are blended and there is no loose flour. You may see some lumps; that's okay. Stir in the chocolate chips.
2. Preheat the oven to 250° F. You will be keeping the first batches of pancakes warm in the oven until all the batter is used.
3. Heat a griddle or frying pan over heat, and add 1 tbsp. of the butter. Using a pastry brush (preferably silicone); spread the butter evenly over the surface. Using 3 tbsp. for each pancake, scoop the batter onto the hot griddle, being careful not to crowd the pancakes. After 3 to 4 mins, when bubbles have formed near the pancakes' edges (they will not bubble in the center), the edges have begun to look dry, and

the underside is golden brown; carefully turn the pancakes with a spatula. Cook until browned, 1½ to 2 mins longer. Shift to a platter in a single layer and place in the oven. Do not cover them. They will become get soggy. Repeat with the remaining batter, adding additional butter to the skillet as needed.

4. Serve the pancakes hot and pass the vanilla yogurt at the table.

19. SEED AND BACON CORNBREAD

YIELD: Makes one piece cornbread |MIXING TIME: 10 mins |**BAKING**: 400°F for about 20 mins

INGREDIENTS

- 1 tsp. baking soda
- ½ tsp. kosher salt
- 1¼ cups fine-or -grind stoneground yellow cornmeal
- 1 cup unbleached all-purpose flour
- ¼ cup granulated sugar
- 2 tsp. baking powder
- 1½ cups buttermilk, any fat content
- One egg
- 2 tbsp. unsalted butter, melted

- Four thick slices of bacon (about 5 oz. total), fried crisp, drained, and broken into pieces
- 1 cup shredded Cheddar cheese

METHOD

1. Preheat the oven to400°F.
2. Butter a 9-in square pan with 2-in sides.
3. Sift together the flour, sugar, baking powder, baking soda, and salt into a bowl. Stir in the cornmeal and set aside. In a bowl, stir together the buttermilk, egg, and melted butter until blended. Pour the flour
4. Mixture over the buttermilk mixture and stir the batter slowly. Stir in the bacon and cheese. Scrape into the prepared pan.
5. Bake until the top feels firm if touched and a toothpick inserted in the center comes out clean, about 20 mins. Let cool in the pan and serve warm.
6. The cornbread can be baked a day ahead, covered, and left at room temperature. Reheat the bread, covered, until warm, about 15 mins.

20.CORNBREAD OOPSIE

YIELD: Makes one square bread |**MIXING TIME:** 10 mins |**BAKING**: 400°F for about 20 mins

INGREDIENTS

- ½ tsp. kosher salt
- 1 cup fine-grind stoneground yellow cornmeal
- 1¼ cups buttermilk, any fat content
- One egg
- 1 tbsp. unsalted butter, plus 4 tbsp. melted butter
- 1 cup unbleached all-purpose flour
- 13 cup granulated sugar
- 2 tsp. baking powder
- 1 tsp. baking soda

METHOD

1. Preheat the oven to400°F. Put the 1 tbsp. butter in an 8-in square pan with 2-in sides. About 2 mines before you are ready to pour the batter into the pan put the pan in the preheated oven to melt the butter.

2. Sift together the flour, sugar, baking powder, baking soda, and salt into a bowl. Stir in the cornmeal and set aside. In a bowl, stir together the buttermilk, egg, and the 4 tbsp. melted butter until blended. Pour the flour mixture over the buttermilk mixture and stir the batter slowly.

3. Remove the pan from the oven and tilt it to coat the bottom and sides with the melted butter. The butter may be browned (this is fine) but should not be burnt. Scrape the batter into the prepared pan.

4. Bake until the top feels firm if touched and a toothpick inserted in the center comes out clean, about 20 mins. Let cool in the pan, then cut into squares and serve warm.

5. The cornbread can be baked a day ahead, covered, and left at room temperature. Reheat the bread, covered, until warm, about 15 mins.

21.COCONUT CLOUD BREAD

YIELD: Makes one bread |MIXING TIME: **10 mins |BAKING**: **425°F for about 15 mins**

INGREDIENTS
- ¼ tsp. kosher salt
- ½ cup buttermilk, any fat content
- One egg
- 2 tbsp. unsalted butter, melted
- 1 tsp. corn or canola oil plus 1 tbsp.
- 2 tbsp. coconut flour
- ¾ cup fine-grind stoneground yellow cornmeal
- 1 tbsp. granulated sugar

- ½ tsp. baking powder
- ½ tsp. baking soda

METHOD

1. Preheat the oven to425°F. Have ready a pan with seven openings.

2. In a pan, melt the butter with 1 tsp. of oil. Use a pastry brush to brush the corn stick pan openings with the butter-oil. Heat the pan in the oven for 5 mins while you mix the batter.

3. In a bowl, stir the flour, cornmeal, sugar, baking soda, and salt. Add the buttermilk, egg, baking powder, and the remaining 1 tbsp. oil and stir the batter slowly. The batter will fill to the rim.

4. Bake until it is browned, and a toothpick inserted in the center of a corn stick comes out clean, about 15 mins. The bottoms of the corn sticks will be browned. Let cool in the pan for 5 mins. Use a sharp knife and your fingers to loosen the sticks' edges and carefully remove the pan's sticks to the rack. Do not want to turn the pan upside down to release the corn sticks because it could weigh them down and break them. Serve warm.

5. The corn sticks can be baked a day ahead, covered, and left at room temperature. Reheat

the sticks, uncovered, until warm, about 10 mins.

22. CARAMELISED APRICOT MUFFINS

YIELD: Makes six muffins |**MIXING TIME: 10 mins** |**BAKING**: 375°F for about 20 mins

INGREDIENTS

- 6 tbsp. unsalted butter, melted
- 13 cup pure maple syrup
- Two eggs
- ½ cup dried apricots, coarsely chopped
- Butter for serving
- 1 cup fine-grind stoneground yellow cornmeal
- 1 cup unbleached all-purpose flour
- 1 tsp. baking powder
- 1 tsp. baking soda
- ½ tsp. kosher salt
- ½ cup whole milk

METHOD

1. Preheat the oven to 375°F.

2. Butter six wells (each with 1-cup capacity) in a jumbo muffin tin.

3. In a bowl, stir the cornmeal, flour, baking powder, baking soda, and salt. In a bowl, stir the milk, butter, maple syrup, and eggs until blended. Stir in the apricot pieces. Pour the flour mixture over the milk mixture, and stir the batter slowly. You will have 3 cups of batter. Pour ½ cup batter into each prepared muffin well.

4. Bake until the tops feel firm if touched and are evenly browned (signaling the sides are browned), and a toothpick inserted in the center of a muffin comes out clean, about 20 mins. Let cool for about 10 mins. Run a knife to loosen the muffin sides, turn the muffins out onto the rack to cool for at least 15 mins. Serve warm or at room temperature with butter.

5. Reheat the muffins, covered, until warm, about 10 mins.

23.CORNMEAL DELIGHT

YIELD: Makes about 20 cornmeals

MIXING TIME: 15 mins

FRYING: About 4 mins per batch at 365°F.

INGREDIENTS

- One yellow onion
- Corn oil for deep-frying
- Kosher or sea salt for finishing
- 1 cup fine-or -grind stoneground yellow cornmeal
- ½ cup unbleached all-purpose flour
- 1½ tsp. baking soda
- ½ tsp. kosher salt
- 1 cup buttermilk, any fat content
- One egg, beaten

METHOD

1. In a bowl, stir together the cornmeal, flour, baking soda, and salt. Stir in the buttermilk and egg just to moisten and blend the ingredients. Stir in the onion.

2. Line a baking sheet with paper towels and place it near the stove. Pour 2 in of oil into a heavy saucepan and heat overheat to 365°F on a deep-frying thermometer. Using a spoon, drop the batter by tablespoons into the hot oil, frying 6 or 7 at a time. The batter will puff and float to the top. Fry until the undersides are browned, about 2 mins. Using a slotted spoon, turn and fry until a deep golden brown, about 2 mins longer. Using the slotted spoon, transfer to the towel-lined pan to drain. Fry the remaining batter the same way in two batches, allowing the oil to return to 365°F before adding each batch. Sprinkle with salt and serve.

24. SPOON BREAD

YIELD: Makes eight servings |MIXING TIME: 15 mins |BAKING: 350°F for about 1 hour

INGREDIENTS

- 1 cup fine-grind stoneground yellow cornmeal
- 2 cups water
- 3 tbsp. unsalted butter, at room temperature
- Four eggs
- 1 tsp. kosher salt
- 1 cup whole milk
- 1 tsp. baking powder
- Butter for serving

METHOD

1. Preheat the oven to 350°F.

2. Butter a soufflé or other round baking dish with a 2-qt capacity.

3. In a heavy saucepan, combine the cornmeal and water, place overheat, and bring to a simmer, beating constantly. Cook, constantly beating, until the mixture thickens for about 3 mins, then beat for 1 minute. There should be only an occasional bubble and never a full boil. Transfer and beat in the butter. It will melt quickly. Scrap the batter into a bowl and let it cools.

4. Using a stand blender fitted with the flat beater, another bowl beat the eggs and salt on speed for 2 mins. At low speed, mix in the milk and baking powder. Slowly add spoonful's (about five additions) of the cornmeal mixture to the batter, incorporating each addition before adding the next one. The batter will be thin, and there will be a few lumps. Scrape into the prepared soufflé dish.

5. Bake until the top is browned in patches, the edges are browned (this makes a nice crisp

contrast to the soft interior), and the center looks set if you give the baking dish a slight jiggle, about 1 hour. It is okay to bake it for an additional 5 mins if you are unsure if it is done. Serve.

25. DARK RYE BREAD

YIELD: Makes one oval loaf MIXING TIME: 10 mins |REFRIGERATOR TIME: Overnight |RISING TIME: 1 hour after refrigeration | BAKING: 350°F for about 35 mins

INGREDIENTS

· 2 cups unbleached all-purpose flour

· 1 tbsp. unsweetened Dutch-process cocoa powder

· 1½ tsp. kosher salt

· 2¼ tsp. instant yeast (one ¼-oz packet)

· 1 cup hot water (about 130°F)

· 2 tbsp. unsulfured light molasses

· 1 cup rye flour

· 1 tbsp. plus 1 tsp. caraway seeds

· Corn or canola oil and stone-ground yellow cornmeal for pan

METHOD

1. In a stand blender fitted with the flat beater, beat together 1 cup of the all-purpose flour, the cocoa powder, salt, and yeast on low speed until combined. Add the hot water and mix until all the ingredients are smoothly combined, then beat for 2 mins. Add the molasses, the remaining 1 cup all-purpose flour, and the rye flour. Continue mixing at low speed for 5 mins, adding the caraway seeds after 4 mins. Stop to scrape down the bowl sides and beater as necessary. The dough will be soft but will come away from the sides of the bowl. The dough is ready if when you stop the blender and stick your

2. Finger into the dough, your finger comes out clean.

3. Transfer the dough to an oiled bowl, and then turn the dough to coat it with oil on both sides. Cover the bowl and refrigerate overnight.

4. Oil about one-third of a baking sheet or about half of a pizza pan, and sprinkle the oiled surface generously with cornmeal. You only

need to oil the part of the pan on which the bread will sit.

5. Remove the dough from the refrigerator, remove the dough from the bowl, and punch it down to press out the air. On a surface, knead the dough into a flat oval about 9 in long. Beginning from a long side, roll up the oval. The loaf will be about 9 in long and narrower at the ends than in the center. The dough is elastic, making it easy to shape. Place the dough roll on the slippery part of the pan.

6. The loaf will raise the only s. When the dough has risen for 40 mins, preheat the oven to 350°F. When the dough has risen for 50 mins, put a clean rock on a metal pie pan and put the pan on the lowest rack of the oven (or, lacking a rock, put the empty pan on the rack).

7. Pour about 2 tbsp. water over the rock in the pie pan to create steam (or directly into the empty pan). Put them in the oven and bake until the top is firm and crusty and the bottom is browned for about 35 mins. The bread will rise about 1 in during baking. Remove from the oven and slide the loaf onto a wire rack to cool

completely. The crust on top will be firm but not exceptionally crisp when cooled.

8. The bread can be baked up to 2 days ahead and stored in a plastic bag at room temperature. Once it is cut, continue to store it in a plastic bag to keep it fresh.

26.PARKER HOUSE ROLLS

YIELD: Makes 18 to 20 rolls

MIXING TIME: 10 mins

REFRIGERATOR TIME: Overnight

RISING TIME: About 30 mins after refrigeration

BAKING: 350°F for about 22 mins

INGREDIENTS

- ½ cup whole milk
- 2 tbsp. unsalted butter
- 3¾ cups unbleached all-purpose flour
- ½ cup granulated sugar
- 1 tsp. kosher salt
- 4½ tsp. active dry yeast (two ¼-oz packets)
- Two eggs
- 1 cup sour cream

- 5½ tbsp. unsalted butter, 3 ½ tbsp. at room temperature, for filling rolls;
- 2 tbsp. unsalted butter, melted, for brushing rolls

METHOD

1. In a pan, heat the milk and butter overheat to about 130°F on an instant-read thermometer. Remove from the heat.

2. In a stand blender fitted with the flat beater, mix 1 cup of the flour, sugar, salt, and yeast on low speed until combined. Add the milk and mix until all the ingredients are smoothly combined, then beat for 2 mins. With the blender still on low speed, add the eggs and sour cream and beat until blended. Add the remaining 2¾ cups flour and continue mixing for 5 mins. Stop to scrape down the bowl sides and beater as necessary. The dough will be very soft but should come away from the sides of the bowl.

3. Transfer the dough to a buttered bowl, and then turn the dough to coat it with butter on both sides. Cover the bowl and refrigerate overnight or up to 2 days. The dough will about

double in size.

4. Line a baking sheet with parchment paper. Rolling out the dough will press out the air, so you don't need to punch it down. Using a 2½-in round biscuit cutter and dipping it in flour before each use, cut out circles. Make a crease in the center or s off-center on each circle. Spread about ½ tsp. of the room-temperature butter on the crease of a circle and fold the dough over itself along the crease. Press at the fold's edges to seal the roll's ends, and gently press to seal the edge along the roll's top. This technique holds the folded top in place and, at the same time, allows it to pull away during baking. Repeat with the remaining circles. Place them on the baking sheet ½ in apart if you want the rolls to touch one another and form soft edges during baking, or 1 in apart if you want the rolls to remain separated and browns on the edges. Then gather the dough scraps and roll and cut to make more rolls. Brush the rolls with 1 tbsp. of the melted butter.

5. Cover the rolls and let rise until s puffed for about 30 mins. The dough will not raise much.

Most of the rising happen during baking. When the rolls have risen for 10 mins, preheat the oven to 350°F.

6. Bake until brown, and the bottoms are browned

7. For about 22 mins. Use a spatula to slide the rolls onto a wire rack, then brush with the remaining 1 tbsp. melted butter. Serve warm or at room temperature.

8. The rolls can be baked up to 2 days ahead, covered, and stored at room temperature. To serve, reheat the rolls, covered, until warm, about 15 mins.

27.ANYTIME BUTTER TWISTS

YIELD: Makes eight twists |MIXING TIME: 10 mins |REFRIGERATOR TIME: **4 hours or up to 4 days |RISING TIME: About 30 mins after refrigeration |BAKING**: **375°F for about 20 mins**

INGREDIENTS

- ¾ cup whole milk
- 2½ cups unbleached all-purpose flour
- 2 tbsp. granulated sugar
- ½ tsp. kosher salt
- 2¼ tsp. active dry yeast (one ¼-oz packet)
- One egg
- ½ cup cold butter, plus 5 tbsp. melted, for brushing twists

METHOD

1. In a saucepan, heat the milk overheat to about 130°F on an instant-read thermometer.

2. In a bowl and a spoon, stir together 1 cup of the flour, sugar, salt, and yeast. Add the milk and stir. Stir in the egg until blended.

3. Put the remaining 1½ cups flour in a bowl and scatter the cold butter pieces over the top. Using your thumb and fingertips, two table knives, or a pastry blender, work the butter into the flour until flour-coated pea-sized pieces form. Stir the butter-flour mixture into the milk mixture until the flour is moistened and a sticky dough forms. You will see pieces of butter; this is good. Cover the bowl for 4 hours or up to 4 days. The dough will about double in size. Once the soft dough is cold, it is easy to roll and twist.

4. If you are baking half of the dough or less, line a baking sheet with parchment paper. If you are baking all of the dough, prepare two baking sheets. Remove half of the dough from the refrigerator. Roll out the dough into a rectangle ten by 4 in and about 3/8 in thick. Rolling out

the dough will press out the air, so you don't need to punch it down. If necessary, pat the dough to make the edges of the rectangle even. Brush with about 1 tbsp. of

5. The melted butter. If desired, sprinkle with one of the seasonings suggested in the introductory note, pressing them onto the dough.

6. Using a sharp knife, cut the dough into four strips, each 1 in wide and 10 in long. Pick up one strip, holding each end with one hand. Twist the ends to create a tightly twisted strip. The dough will stretch about 1 in as you twist it to make a twist 11 in long. Place the twist on a prepared baking sheet. Repeat with the three remaining strips and add to the baking sheet, spacing them 2 in apart. Brush the twists with some of the melted butter. Roll out and shape the remaining half of the dough the same way, place on the second prepared sheet, and brush with the remaining butter. Or, cover the remaining dough, pressing the wrap directly onto the surface and leaving it in the refrigerator to shape another day. Keeping in mind, you must use it within four days of when

it was first refrigerated.

7. Cover the buttered twists and let rise until s puffed for about 30 mins. The dough will not raise much. Most of the rising happen during baking. When the dough has risen for 10 mins, preheat the oven to375°F.

8. Bake the twists one sheet at a time until the tops are browned, and the bottoms are browned for about 20 mins. Let cool on the pan for 15 mins. Serve warm.

9. The twists can be baked up to 2 days ahead, covered, and stored at room temperature. To serve, reheat the twists until warm, about 15 mins.

28. CINNAMON TWISTS

YIELD: Makes 12 twists |MIXING TIME: 15 mins for dough and filling |REFRIGERATOR TIME: **Overnight or up to 3 days |RISING TIME: About 40 mins after refrigeration |BAKING: 375°F for about 40 mins**

INGREDIENTS

- ½ recipe (21 oz.) Sweet Dough for Extra-Sticky Caramel-Pecan Buns
- 2 tbsp. unsalted butter, melted
- ½ cup granulated sugar mixed with 1 tsp. ground cinnamon

METHOD

1. Make the dough and refrigerate as directed.
2. Butter a 9-in square or 11-by-7-in pan.
3. Roll out the dough into a 12-in square. Rolling out the dough will press out the air, so you don't need to punch it down. Brush the dough with 1 tbsp. of the melted butter. Sprinkle ¼ cup of the cinnamon sugar over the dough, leaving a ½-in border uncovered on all sides. Fold one-third of the dough over onto the square. Brush the folded portion with some of the remaining melted butter, and then sprinkle the remaining cinnamon sugar over the buttered surface. Now, fold the two dough layers to meet the original dough square's bottom edge and press to seal all the edges. You will have a three-layered strip that measures 12 in long and about 4 in wide.
4. Cut the dough strip crosswise into twelve equal pieces, each about 1 in wide.
5. Pick up one strip, holding each end with one hand. Twist the ends in to create a tightly twisted strip. Repeat to make five more twists, and then place the six twists in a row along the

prepared pan's top half; they will just touch. Repeat with the remaining strips and place in a row along the bottom half of the pan. Brush the twists' tops with the remaining melted butter and sprinkle any cinnamon sugar that fell out of the twists during shaping and transferring. Some of the sugar will fall onto the pan's bottom and form a light glaze during baking.

6. Cover the twists and let rise until puffy, about 40 mins. The dough will not double in size. When the twists have risen for 20 mins, preheat the oven to375°F.

7. Bake the twists until the edges and tops are browned, about 40 mins. They will spread into a single, pull-apart cake as they bake. Let cool on the pan for 5 mins. Use a sharp knife to loosen the twists from the sides of the pan. Invert a wire rack on top of the pan, and holding the rack and pan firmly together with potholders, invert them together. Carefully lift off the pan. Invert a second wire rack on top of the twists, invert the racks together, and lift off the top rack. The twists are now right-side up. Let cool for at least 15 mins before serving. To serve,

cut, or pull apart.

8. The twists can be covered and stored at room temperature overnight. To serve, preheat the oven to oven to 250°F and reheat the twists, covered, until warm, about 15 mins.

29.SALLY LUNN BREAD

YIELD: Makes one round or two loaves |MIXING TIME: 10 mins |RESTING TIME: 10 mins | RISING TIME: About 1 hour |BAKING:375°F for about 50 mins

INGREDIENTS

1¼ cups milk, any fat content

½ cup unsalted butter

4 cups unbleached all-purpose flour

13 cup granulated sugar

1 tsp. kosher salt

2¼ tsp. instant yeast (one ¼-oz packet)

Three eggs

METHOD

1. Butter the bottom, sides, and tube of a 9½-or 10-in tube pan with at least 3¾-insides and a fixed bottom. Line the pan with butter the paper. Or, butter two 9-by-5-by-3-in loaf pans, line the bottoms with parchment, and butter the paper.

2. In a pan, heat the butter and milk overheat to about 130°F on an instant-read thermometer. Remove from the heat.

3. In a stand blender fitted with the flat beater, mix 1 cup of the flour, sugar, salt, and yeast on low speed until combined. Add the milk and mix until all the ingredients are smoothly combined.

4. Add the eggs and mix, then continue to beat for 1 minute. Add the remaining 3 cups flour and continue mixing for 6 mins. The dough will be sticky and will not come away from the sides of the bowl. Scrape the dough into the prepared pan(s).

5. Cover the pan(s) and let the dough rise for about 1 hour. The dough will rise about halfway up the sides of the pan(s). When the dough has

risen for 40 mins, preheat the oven to375°F.

6. Bake the bread until the top feels firm and the top and sides are browned for about 50 mins. The bread will rise to at least the top of the pan(s).

30. LOTS OF CHEESE BREAD

YIELD: Makes one loaf |**MIXING TIME**: 10 mins | **RISING TIME: About 45 mins** |**BAKING: 375°F for about 45 mins**

INGREDIENTS

- Unsalted butter for pan
- 1 cup whole milk
- 2¾ cups unbleached all-purpose flour
- 1 tbsp. granulated sugar
- ½ tsp. kosher salt
- 2¼ tsp. instant yeast (one ¼-oz packet)
- One egg
- 8 oz. sharp Cheddar cheese, cut into ½-to ¾-in pieces

METHOD

Butter a 9-by-5-by-3-in loaf pan (or another loaf pan with an 8-cup capacity). Line the bottom of the pan with parchment paper.

In a saucepan, heat the milk overheat to about 130°F on an instant-read thermometer. Remove from the heat.

In a stand blender fitted with the flat beater, mix 1 cup of the flour, sugar, salt, and yeast on low speed until combined. Add the hot milk and mix until smoothly combined. Add the egg and continue beating for 2 mins. Add the remaining 1¾ cups flour and continue mixing for 5 mins. The dough will be soft and will come away from the sides of the bowl, and if you stop the blender and stick a finger into the dough, your finger will come out clean.

. Sprinkle the cheese pieces evenly over the top. Using the heel of one hand, push the dough down and away against the surface. Then, using your fingertips, fold it toward you. Rotate the dough a quarter turn and repeat the pushing and folding about five times. Several pieces of cheese will poke out of the dough. This is fine. The dough will firm s as the cheese is worked into it. The loaf will not fill the pan.

Let the dough rise to within 1 in the pan's top, about 45 mins. When the dough has risen for 25 mins, preheat the oven to375°F.

Bake the bread until the top feels firm and is browned for about 45 mins. Let cool in the pan for 10 mins. Run a sharp knife around the pan's inside edge to loosen the bread sides, and then turn the bread out onto the rack. Let cool completely.

The bread can be stored in a plastic bag at room temperature for up to 3 days.

31. CARROT, CRANBERRY & WALNUT LOAF

YIELD: Makes one loaf |MIXING TIME: 10 minutes |BAKING: 350°F for about 55 minutes

INGREDIENTS

- 1 cup unbleached all-purpose flour
- 1 cup whole-wheat flour
- 1 cup granulated sugar
- 1 tsp. baking powder
- 1 tsp. ground cinnamon
- ¼ tsp. kosher salt
- 3 large eggs, lightly beaten
- ¾ cup corn or canola oil
- 1½ cups coarsely grated carrots
- 1 tsp. pure vanilla extract
- ½ tsp. finely grated, peeled fresh ginger

- ¾ cup coarsely chopped walnuts
- ¾ cup cranberries, coarsely chopped

METHOD

1. Preheat the oven to 350°F. Butter a pan. Line the pan with parchment paper.

2. In a bowl, mix both flours, sugar, baking powder, cinnamon, and salt. Add the eggs, oil, carrots, vanilla, and ginger and stir until completely incorporated with the flour mixture. Stir in the walnuts and cranberries. Scrape the batter into the prepared pan.

3. Bake until the top feels firm if lightly touched, and a toothpick inserted in the center comes out clean, about 55 mins. Let cool for about 10 mins. Run a knife through the pan to loosen the bread sides, and then turn the bread out onto the rack. Peel off the parchment. Let cool completely.

4. The carrot bread can be wrapped in plastic wrap and stored at room temperature for up to 3 days.

32. DARK IRISH SODA BREAD

YIELD: It makes one 8-in oval loaf. |**MIXING TIME: 10 minutes** |**BAKING: 375°F for about 35 minutes**

INGREDIENTS

- 1½ cups whole-wheat flour
- ¾ cup unbleached all-purpose flour
- 1 tbsp. packed brown sugar
- 2 tsp. caraway seeds
- 1 tsp. baking soda
- ½ tsp. kosher salt
- 2 tbsp. unsalted butter, melted
- 1 tbsp. unsulfured light molasses
- 1 cup buttermilk, any fat content

METHOD

1. Preheat the oven to 375°F.

2. Butter a baking sheet and sprinkle it lightly with whole-wheat flour.

3. In a stand blender fitted with the flat beater, mix both flours, the brown sugar, caraway seeds, baking soda, and salt on low speed until combined. Add the melted butter and mix until blended. Stir the molasses into the buttermilk, add to the flour mixture, and continue mixing at low speed until soft dough forms, about 1 minute.

4. Take the dough into a ball and roll it around between your palms to smooth it as much as possible. It will not be perfectly smooth. Form into an 8-in-long oval by patting it gently and place on the prepared pan. Use a sharp knife to cut a Lengthwise slash about 5 in long and ¼ in deep along the center of the loaf.

5. Bake the bread until it feels firm and crisp, and the bottom is browned if you lift it carefully, about 35 minutes. Let cool on the pan for 10 minutes; then slide onto the rack and let cool completely.

CONCLUSION

Keto bread may not be as rich in other nutrients that are found in whole grains, such as B vitamins and minerals. You can, of course, make your keto bread, and many die-hard keto dietitians advise going this r oute so you can control what goes into your loaf. The major plus of keto bread: It allows keto dieters to eat bread. For keto dieters, bread and bagels are typically off-limits. We are now seeing an explosion in keto-friendly product innovation, where popular carb-rich foods are substituted for low-carb alternatives. Bread is undoubtedly one of those foods, giving people the option to enjoy their favorite foods, not feel deprived, and still meet their carb budget. I am sure that you will enjoy my recipes!

KETO CHAFFLESS RECIPES

Table of content

1.

INTRODUCTION

You know how sometimes you go to bed with something on your mind and you think maybe a good night's sleep will clear your head? For me, that something was chaffless. Well, it was anything but chaffless. I already knew waffle batter would work in the waffle iron, but I caught little glimpses of other things: a French toast recipe for the chaffle iron . . . cookies with a waffle pattern on them ...waffled bacon. It wasn't much to go on, but it was enough. I was obsessed. What else would work in the waffle iron? The idea wouldn't quit me on its own, so I decided to do something about it. In the proud tradition—well, the tradition—of people with too much time on their hands, I took my obsession to the Internet and created the blog Waffleizer. Once the "Will It chaffle?" question was out there, people were hungry for answers. Suddenly, the humble waffle iron was capable of more than most people had imagined. Once, it was for making waffles. Now it was for making breakfast, lunch, dinner, and everything in between.

Forgotten waffle irons emerged from dusty cabinets. Neglected waffle makers earned permanent space on the counter. A breakfast specialist turned into an all-day multi tasker. And I heard about it all. People wrote to tell me that I had made them fall in love with their waffle irons all over again. (What had caused the falling out in the first place?) They wrote to tell me they were seriously thinking about getting a waffle iron. (Really? Just seriously thinking about it? How about seriously doing it?) They wrote to suggest recipes. There's something about waffle geometry and the waffle iron's transformative power that turns a recipe into an adventure. If there's one thing that's become clear to me, it's that I'm not the only one who finds the adventure irresistible.

BREAKFAST AND BRUNCH

33.Crispy Waffled Bacon and Eggs

IRON: Belgian or standard | TIME: 10 minutes | YIELD: Serves 2

INGREDIENTS

- Four strips bacon
- Two large eggs
- Salt and freshly ground black pepper, to taste

DIRECTIONS

1. Preheat the waffle iron. Preheat the oven on its Lowest setting. Line a plate with paper towels.

2. Place the bacon strips in the waffle iron and close the lid. Make sure the bacon is not hanging out of the sides of the waffle iron.

3. Check after 4 minutes. Thin-cut bacon could be ready, though thicker cuts may need another 1 to 2 minutes. Bacon is ready when it is crispy without being blackened.

4. Remove the bacon and drain it on the paper towel–lined plate to absorb some of the greases.

5. Crack the eggs into a small bowl. This will give you control over how the eggs land on the waffle iron. The waffle iron should be well greased from cooking the bacon, but if necessary, use a silicone pastry brush to distribute the bacon fat evenly across the waffle iron portion where the eggs will cook.

6. Pour the eggs onto the greased part of the waffle iron. Cook, without closing the lid, until the egg white has set, about a minute, and continue cooking until the yolk has set a bit, 1

or 2 minutes more.

7. To remove the eggs intact, use an offset spatula or a pair of heat-resistant silicone spatulas to coax them from the waffle iron grid. Loosen the edges first and then lift out the egg while supporting it from below as much as possible.

8. Season with salt and pepper and serve with the waffled bacon.

34. Sweet and Savory Waffled Sausage Patties

IRON: Belgian or standard | TIME: 15 minutes | YIELD: Serves 6

INGREDIENTS

- Two tablespoons maple syrup
- One teaspoon dried sage.
- One teaspoon salt
- ½teaspoon freshly ground black pepper
- ¼ teaspoon dried marjoram ⅛ teaspoon cayenne pepper 1 pound ground pork Nonstick cooking spray

DIRECTIONS

1. Preheat the waffle iron on medium. Preheat the oven on its lowest setting.

2. In a medium-size bowl, combine the maple syrup, sage, salt, black pepper, marjoram, and cayenne pepper and mix well to combine.

3. Add the pork to the spice mixture and mix well with your hands. Form patties that will fit on one section of your waffle iron.

4. Coat both sides of the waffle iron grid with nonstick spray. Place a patty on each section of the waffle iron and close the lid. With thin patties in a conventional-style waffle iron, the meat may be done in as little as 2 minutes. Belgian-style machines or thicker patties may require more time. The pork should reach an internal temperature of 160°F on an Instant-read thermometer.

5. Remove the patties from the Waffle iron and serve. Place the finished sausage patties in the oven to keep them warm while. The others cook in the waffle iron.

35.Waffled Chocolate-Stuffed French Toast with Whipped Butter

IRON: Belgian or standard | TIME: 20 minutes | YIELD: Serves 2

INGREDIENTS

- Two large eggs
- ¼teaspoon pure vanilla extract
- Pinch of salt
- Four slices of bread, such as challah or brioche, cut thick.
- Nonstick cooking spray
- ½ cup chocolate chips (semisweet, bittersweet, or milk chocolate)
- One tablespoon Whipped Butter (recipe follows)
- Powdered sugar, to taste

DIRECTIONS

1. Preheat the waffle iron on high. Preheat the oven on its lowest setting.
2. In a pie pan or deep dish, whisk together the eggs, milk, vanilla, and salt.
3. Place two slices of bread in the egg mixture and soak them until they've absorbed some of the liquid, 30 seconds. Flip the slices and soak them for another 30 seconds.
4. Coat both sides of the waffle iron grid with nonstick spray. Place a slice of soaked bread on the waffle iron and pile a little less than half of the chocolate chips on the slice. Top with the second slice of soaked bread, close the waffle iron, and cook.Until the bread is golden brown and the chocolate is melted 3 to 4 minutes. There should be no trace of the uncooked egg mixture.
5. Remove the French toast from the waffle iron and repeat Steps 3 and 4 to make the second batch. Place the finished French toast in the oven to keep it warm.

6. Slice the French toast into quarters. Pop open the "pocket" in each quarter and stuff the remaining chocolate chips into the opening. The residual heat will melt the chocolate.

7. Top each portion with the Whipped Butter and dust with the powdered sugar before serving.Add more chocolate. A few chocolate chips stuffed into the pocket of the finished product melt in no time from the residual heat.The French toast comes out gorgeously gooey, rich, and delicious.

36.Blueberry Cinnamon Muffles (Waffled Muffins)

IRON: Belgian or standard TIME: 20 minutes YIELD: About 16 muffles

INGREDIENTS

- Two large eggs
- ¼teaspoon pure vanilla extract
- Pinch of salt
- Four slices of bread, such as challah or brioche, cut thick.
- Nonstick cooking spray
- ½ cup chocolate chips (semisweet, bittersweet, or milk chocolate)
- One tablespoon Whipped Butter (recipe follows)
- Powdered sugar, to taste
- 2 cups all-purpose flour

DIRECTIONS

1. Preheat the waffle iron on medium.

2. In a medium-size bowl, combine the flour, sugar, cinnamon, salt, and baking powder.

3. In a large bowl, combine the milk, butter, and eggs and whisk until thoroughly combined.

4. Add the dry ingredients to the milk mixture and whisk until just combined.

5. Fold in the blueberries and stir gently to distribute them evenly.

6. Coat both sides of the waffle iron grid with nonstick spray and pour about 1⁄4 cup of the mixture into each section of the waffle iron. Close the lid and cook for 4 minutes, or until just golden brown.

7. Remove the muffles from the waffle iron and let them cool slightly on a wire rack. Repeat Step 6 with the remaining batter.

8. Serve warm.

37. Waffled Ham and Cheese Melt with Maple Butter

IRON: Belgian or standard | TIME: 10 minutes | YIELD: Serves 1

INGREDIENTS

- One tablespoon unsalted butter, at room temperature
- Two slices sandwich bread
- 2 ounces Gruyère cheese, sliced
- 3 ounces Black Forest ham, sliced
- One tablespoon Maple Butter (recipe follows)

DIRECTIONS

1. Preheat the waffle iron on low.

2. Spread a thin, even layer of butter on one side of each piece of bread.

3. Pile the cheese and ham on the unbuttered side of one slice of bread and put the open-face sandwich in the waffle iron as far away from the hinge as possible. (This allows the lid to press down on the sandwich more evenly.) Place the second slice of bread on top, with the buttered side up, and close the waffle iron.

4. Check the sandwich after 3 minutes. About halfway through, you may need to rotate the sandwich 180 degrees to ensure even pressure and cooking. If you'd like, you can press down on the lid of the waffle iron a bit to compact the sandwich, but do so carefully— the lid could be very hot. Remove the sandwich from the waffle iron when the bread is golden brown, and the cheese is melted.

5. Spread the Maple Butter on the outside of the sandwich. Slice in half diagonally and serve.

38.Waffled Hash Browns with Rosemary

IRON: Belgian or standard | TIME: 20 minutes | YIELD: Serves 2

INGREDIENTS

- One russet (baking) potato, about 10 ounces, peeled and shredded
- ½teaspoon finely chopped fresh Rosemary or one teaspoon dried rosemary
- ¼ teaspoon salt
- ½teaspoon freshly ground black pepper

DIRECTIONS

1. Preheat the waffle iron on medium.

2. Squeeze the shredded potato with a towel until it's as dry as you can manage. (Excess liquid is the enemy of crispiness; your potatoes will steam if they aren't dried well.)

3. In a mixing bowl, combine the shredded potato, Rosemary, salt, and pepper.

4. With a silicone brush, spread the butter on both sides of the waffle iron.

5. Pile the shredded potatoes into the waffle iron— overstuff the waffle iron a bit—and close One teaspoon unsalted butter, melted.

6. Grated cheese, sour cream, or ketchup for serving the lid. (The pressure of the lid will compress the potatoes and help them emerge as a cohesive, waffled unit.)

7. After 2 minutes, press down a bit on the lid to further compress the potatoes. (Careful: The lid may be hot.) Check the potatoes after 10 minutes. They should be just starting to turn golden brown in places.

8. When the potatoes are golden brown throughout, 1 to 2 minutes more, carefully

remove them from the waffle iron.

9. Serve with grated cheese, sour cream, or ketchup.

39. Truffled Eggs, Scrambled and Waffled

IRON: Belgian or standard | TIME: 5 minutes | YIELD: Serves 1

INGREDIENTS

- Two large eggs
- One tablespoon heavy (whipping) cream
- One teaspoon black truffle-infused oil
- Pinch of salt
- Pinch of freshly ground black pepper
- One tablespoon melted butter for brushing waffle iron.

DIRECTIONS

1. Preheat the waffle iron on medium.

2. In a medium-size bowl, whisk the eggs with the cream until just combined

3. Add the truffle oil, salt, and pepper, and whisk again to combine.

4. Use a silicone brush to generously coat the bottom grid of the waffle iron with butter.

5. Pour the eggs onto the waffle iron and leave the lid open.

6. Using a silicone spatula, stir the eggs frequently while they cook. The trick here is to move.

7. The eggs out of the crevices so that the uncooked egg can come into contact with the waffle iron and cook thoroughly.

8. Keep a close eye on the eggs. They may be done in as little as 2 minutes, though they may take up to 3 minutes. No runny parts should remain.Remove the eggs from the waffle iron with an offset spatula or a pair of heat-resistant silicone spatulas. Loosen the edges first and then lift out the eggs while supporting them from below as much as possible. Serve hot.

LUNCH RECIPES

40. Gridded Grilled Cheese

IRON: Belgian or standard | TIME: 5 minutes | YIELD: Serves 1

INGREDIENTS

- One tablespoon unsalted butter, at room temperature
- 2 slices sturdy sandwich bread
- 3 ounces cheese, such as Cheddar or

DIRECTIONS

1. Preheat the waffle iron on low.
2. Butter one side of each slice of bread.
3. Place a slice of bread, buttered side down, on the waffle iron, as far away from the hinge as possible. (This will allow the lid to press down on the sandwich more evenly.) Distribute the cheese evenly on the bread. Top with the second slice of bread, buttered side up.
4. Close the lid of the waffle iron and cook until the cheese is melted and the bread is golden brown, 3 minutes. About halfway through, you may need to rotate the sandwich 180 degrees to ensure even pressure and cooking.
5. Remove the sandwich from the waffle iron. Slice into halves or quarters and serve.

41.Green Chile Waffled Quesadillas

IRON: Belgian or standard | TIME: 10 minutes | YIELD: Makes two quesadillas

INGREDIENTS

- Nonstick cooking spray four flour tortillas
- 1 cup shredded Mexican-style cheese, such as queso Chihuahua or Monterey Jack
- ¼ cup chopped canned green chiles

DIRECTIONS

1. Preheat the waffle iron on medium. Coat both sides of the waffle iron grid with nonstick spray.

2. Place a tortilla on the waffle iron and, taking care because the waffle iron is hot, spread half of the cheese and half of the green chiles evenly across the tortilla, leaving a margin of an inch or so around the edge of the tortilla. Top with another tortilla and close the waffle iron.

3. Check the quesadilla after 3 minutes. When the cheese is melted, and the tortilla has golden brown waffle marks, it is ready. Remove the quesadilla from the waffle iron.

4. Repeat Steps 2 and 3 with the remaining ingredients, cut into wedges and serve.

42.WBLT (Waffled Bacon, Lettuce, and Tomato)

IRON: Belgian or standard | TIME: 10 minutes | YIELD: Serves 1

INGREDIENTS

- Three strips bacon
- Two teaspoons mayonnaise
- One small ripe tomato, cut into ½-inch-thick slices.
- One tablespoon unsalted butter, at room temperature
- Two slices sturdy sandwich

DIRECTIONS

1. Preheat the waffle iron on medium.

2. Place the bacon strips in the waffle iron and close the lid. To ensure the bacon cooks thoroughly and evenly, make sure no part of the bacon is hanging out of the waffle iron.

3. After 4 minutes, check the bacon—thin-cut slices could be ready, though thicker cuts may need 1 or 2 minutes more. When the bacon is crispy without being blackened, remove it from the waffle iron and set it aside. Turn the waffle iron down to low.

4. Spread a thin, even layer of butter on one side of each piece of bread. Spread the mayonnaise on the other side of one slice of bread and place it—mayo side up—on the waffle bread. Two leaves of lettuce washed and dried completely iron, as far away from the hinge as possible. (This allows the lid to press down on the sandwich more evenly.) Distribute the bacon, tomato, and lettuce evenly across the sandwich. Top with the second slice of bread, butter side up.

5. Close the lid of the waffle iron and cook until the bread. It is golden brown, 2 minutes. You may need to rotate the sandwich 180 degrees about halfway to ensure even Pressure and cooking.
6. Remove the sandwich, slice it is half diagonally, and serves.

43. Waffled Cuban sandwich

IRON: Belgian or standard | TIME: 10 minutes | YIELD: Serves 2

INGREDIENTS

- One crusty sandwich roll or individual ciabatta loaf
- One tablespoon yellow mustard
- 3 ounces cooked ham, thinly sliced
- 3 ounces cooked pork loin, thinly sliced
- 3 ounces Swiss cheese, thinly sliced
- Two dill pickles, thinly sliced lengthwise

DIRECTIONS

1. Preheat the waffle iron on low.

2. Split the bread into top and bottom halves, hollow it out a bit to make room for the meat, and spread the mustard across both slices. Assemble the ham, pork loin, cheese, and pickles between the pieces of bread.

3. Press down on the sandwich to compact it slightly and place it in the waffle iron, as far away from the hinge as possible. (This allows the lid to press down on the sandwich more evenly.)

4. Close the lid of the waffle iron and cook for 5 minutes. You may need to rotate the sandwich 180 degrees about halfway to ensure even pressure and cooking. If you'd like, you can press down on the waffle iron lid a bit to compact the sandwich, but do so carefully—the lid could be very hot.

5. Remove the sandwich from the waffle iron when the cheese is thoroughly melted. Cut the sandwich in half, or diagonally, and serve.

44. Waffled Gyro with Tzatziki Sauce

IRON: Belgian or standard | TIME: 45 minutes | YIELD: Serves 4

INGREDIENTS

Tzatziki sauce:

- Two cloves garlic, finely minced
- 16 ounces plain Greek yogurt
- One medium-size cucumber, peeled, seeded, and finely chopped.
- One tablespoon extra-virgin olive oil
- Two teaspoons white vinegar Pinch of kosher salt

Gyros:

- One tablespoon dried parsley
- One teaspoon chili powder
- One teaspoon ground coriander

- One teaspoon ground cumin
- One teaspoon dried oregano.
- One teaspoon dried thyme.
- ½ teaspoon paprika
- ½ teaspoon garlic powder
- ½ teaspoon ground cinnamon
- ½ teaspoon salt
- 1 pound lean ground lamb Nonstick cooking spray four pita bread pockets
- One medium-size tomato, cut into cubes.
- One medium-size onion, thinly sliced

DIRECTIONS

1. Make the sauce: In a medium-size bowl, combine half of the garlic with the remaining ingredients and stir well. Taste and add more garlic, if desired. Refrigerate the sauce for at least 30 minutes while you prepare the gyros.
2. Preheat the waffle iron on medium.
3. Make the gyros: In a large bowl, combine the parsley, chili powder, coriander, cumin, oregano, thyme, paprika, garlic powder, cinnamon, and salt, and then add the meat to the spice mixture. Mix well to distribute the

spices evenly.

4. Form the spiced lamb into four patties. Coat both sides of the waffle iron grid with nonstick spray.

5. Place a patty on the waffle iron, close the lid, and cook until no pink traces remain 4 minutes. If you're using an instant-read thermometer, the internal temperature of the lamb should reach 160°F. Repeat for the remaining patties.

6. When all of the lamb patties have finished cooking, warm the pita bread for 15 seconds in the waffle iron.

7. Stuff the warmed pita bread with the lamb, tomato, onion, and tzatziki sauce. Serve with more sauce on the side.

45.Waffled Croque Madame

IRON: Belgian or standard TIME: 5 hours YIELD: Serves up to 6

INGREDIENTS

For 1 Croque Madame:

- One-piece crescent dough (from a tube of prepared crescent rolls) or Brioche Dough (recipe follows)
- One tablespoon unsalted butter, melted.

DIRECTIONS

1. Preheat the waffle iron on medium.
2. IF YOU'RE USING CRESCENT DOUGH: The dough will likely come out of the tube in a wedge shape, but it can be assembled into a square. Cut the wedge of dough in half to make two triangles. Shape the triangles into a square 4 to 5 inches on each side and press the edges together gently. Using a silicone brush, coat both sides of one section of the waffle iron with the melted butter, place the dough on that section of the waffle iron, close the lid, and cook the dough until it is golden brown, about 5 minutes.
3. Remove the dough from the waffle iron and transfer it to a cutting board or plate. Using a silicone brush, coat both sides of one section of the waffle iron with the melted butter and cook the dough on one section of The waffle iron with the lid closed until the dough is golden brown, about 4 minutes. Remove the dough from the waffle iron and transfer it to a cutting board or plate.

4. Pour the Béchamel Sauce onto the waffled dough. (The sauce will mostly pool in the divots.) Then layer the ham on top. Sprinkle the shredded cheese on top. Place the assembled stack in the waffle iron and close the lid for 10 seconds to melt the cheese and marry the layers. Remove the stack from the waffle iron.

5. Crack an egg into a small cup or ramekin. This will give you control over how the egg lands on the waffle iron. Brush the remaining melted butter on the lower grid of one section of the waffle iron and pour the egg onto that section. Cook, without closing the lid, until the white.

46.Béchamel Sauce

INGREDIENTS

- Three tablespoons Béchamel Sauce (recipe follows)
- Two slices of the Black Forest ham
- ¼ cup shredded Gruyère cheese
- One large egg
- Two teaspoons mayonnaise
- One small ripe tomato, cut into ½-inch-thick slices.
- 1 cup milk
- Two tablespoons unsalted butter
- Two tablespoons flour
- ¼ teaspoon salt
- Freshly ground black pepper, to taste.
- Pinch of grated nutmeg

DIRECTIONS

1. Bring the milk to room temperature in a small saucepan over low heat or in the microwave for 45 seconds.

2. Melt the butter in a small saucepan over medium-low heat. Add the flour to the melted butter, constantly whisking until it darkens slightly, 2 minutes.

3. Whisk in the milk in 2 batches, waiting until the mixture is thoroughly combined before adding the second half. Whisk constantly over medium-low heat until the mixture thickens to thick cream consistency, about 5 minutes. Add the salt and a pinch each of pepper and nutmeg, then taste to check the seasoning.

47.Classic Waffleburger with Cheese

IRON: Belgian or standard | TIME: 20 minutes with store-bought buns | YIELD: Serves 4

INGREDIENTS

- Nonstick cooking spray 1 pound ground beef
- ½ teaspoon salt
- One teaspoon freshly ground black pepper.
- Four slices American, Cheddar, or Gruyère cheese (optional)
- Four store-bought or homemade hamburger buns
- Ketchup, mustard, lettuce, tomato, and pickles, for serving

DIRECTIONS

1. Preheat the waffle iron on medium. Coat both sides of the waffle iron grid with nonstick spray.
2. Season the beef with salt and pepper and form it into four patties, each roughly the buns' shape.
3. Place as many patties as will fit in the waffle iron, close the lid, and cook until the beef reaches an internal temperature of 160°F on an instant-read thermometer, 3 minutes.
4. When the patties have cooked, remove them from the waffle iron. If you would like a waffle burger with cheese, leave a patty in the waffle iron, top with the cheese, and close the lid to waffle very briefly— about 5 seconds.
5. Repeat Steps 3 and 4 with any remaining patties.
6. Serve on a bun with ketchup, mustard, lettuce, tomato, and pickles.

DINNER

48.   Waffled Tuna Niçoise Salad

IRON: Belgian or standard | TIME: 45 minutes | YIELD: Serves 2

INGREDIENTS

- Two large eggs
- ½ cup green beans, with tips, snipped
- Four new potatoes, cut in half Salt
- Nonstick cooking spray
- One fresh tuna steak (about 8 ounces)
- 3 cups washed salad greens

- ¼cup pitted or whole sliced black olives, such as Niçoise or kalamata
- ½ cup whole or halved cherry or grape tomatoes
- Freshly ground black pepper, to taste.
- Dijon Vinaigrette Dressing

DIRECTIONS

1. Cook the eggs: Place the eggs in a small saucepan and fill it two-thirds full with water. Bring the water to a boil over medium-high heat, turn off the heat, remove the saucepan from the burner, and cover it. Let it rest for 10 minutes. Run the eggs under cold water for a minute to cool them, and set them aside.

2. Blanch the green beans: Bring a small saucepan of salted water to a boil, and plunge the green beans in for 30 seconds. Remove them and place them in an ice-water bath to stop the cooking. Remove the green beans from the ice water after 1 minute and set aside.

3. Boil the potatoes: Place the potatoes in a small saucepan and cover with at least an inch of water. Add a generous pinch of salt to the water

and bring to a boil over medium-high heat. Once the water boils, reduce the heat to low and allow the potatoes to simmer for 10 minutes. They're ready when they can be pierced with the gentle poke of a knife. Remove the potatoes, drain them in a colander, and let cool.

4. Preheat the waffle iron on high. Coat both sides of the waffle iron grid with nonstick spray.

5. Place the tuna steak on the waffle iron as far away from the hinge as possible. (This allows the lid to press down on the tuna more evenly.) Close the lid.

6. While the tuna cooks, lay down a bed of salad greens on a large serving plate. Peel the eggs, slice or quarter them, and arrange them on the lettuce. Evenly distribute the green beans, potatoes, olives, and tomatoes on the salad greens.

7. Check on the tuna. After Six minutes, a 3⁄4-inch-thick steak should be cooked through. There should be no pink on the exterior. You may wish to cut the tuna in half to see if any pink remains in the center. A pink tinge can be

okay, though you may prefer your tuna better done. (The USDA recommends that it reach 145°F on an instant-read thermometer; I like mine around 125°F.)

8. Remove the tuna from the waffle iron and cut it into slices about 1⁄2 inch thick. Arrange the slices on the salad, with the waffle marks facing up.

9. Sprinkle the salad with salt and pepper. Dress the salad sparingly. Serve the rest of the Dressing at the table.

49.Waffled Salmon with Miso-Maple Glaze and Asparagus

IRON: Belgian or standard | TIME: 15 minutes | YIELD: Serves 2

INGREDIENTS

- One tablespoon maple syrup
- ginger
- asparagus
- salmon
- salt and pepper

DIRECTIONS

1. In a small bowl, whisk together the maple syrup, miso, vinegar, sesame oil, ginger, and garlic. Set the mixture aside.

2. Preheat the waffle iron on high. Coat both sides of the waffle iron grid with nonstick spray.

3. Place the salmon (skin-side down, if it has skin) on the waffle iron and close the lid. While the fish is cooking, toss the asparagus with the olive oil and season with salt and pepper in another bowl.

4. After 4 minutes, check on the fish. The salmon should be close to done. You should see no translucence on the edges. If your fillets are thicker than 1/2 inch or you're unsure whether the salmon is done, use a small, sharp knife to cut a small incision in the middle of the salmon. You should see only a trace of translucence in the middle. (The USDA recommends it reach an internal temperature of 145°F as measured on an instant-read thermometer; I like mine about 135°F.)

5. Use a silicone brush to baste the salmon with the glaze, close the lid, and cook until the glaze

becomes sticky, 1 minute more.

6. Remove the fish from the waffle iron, place the asparagus spears in the waffle iron, and close the lid.

7. Cook the asparagus until just tender, 3 minutes. Thinner spears will finish cooking first. Remove the spears as they finish.

8. Serve the asparagus alongside the salmon. If you have an extra glaze, strain the garlic from it and serve it on the side or drizzle it over the fish.

50. Waffled Calamari Salad with Thai Dressing

IRON: Standard TIME: 10 minutes YIELD: Serves 2

INGREDIENTS

- Nonstick cooking spray
- 8 ounces cleaned squid, bodies, and tentacles
- ½ small red onion, thinly sliced
- Two tablespoons roasted peanuts, crushed.
- Thai Dressing (recipe follows)
- One sprig of cilantro, large stems removed, for garnish
- Thai bird chile peppers or other small chile peppers, for garnish (optional)

DIRECTIONS

1. Preheat the waffle iron on high.

2. Coat both sides of the waffle iron grid with nonstick spray. Arrange the squid on the waffle iron without crowding, close the lid, and cook until the squid is opaque for about 2 minutes.

3. When the squid has finished cooking, allow them to cool slightly on a cutting board, and then cut the bodies into strips about 1 inch wide. The tentacles can remain whole.

4. To serve, arrange the squid on a plate with the onion slices, top with the crushed peanuts, and drizzle with the Thai Dressing. Garnish with cilantro and chiles.

51. Thai Dressing

INGREDIENTS

- Two tablespoons lime juice
- Two tablespoons fish sauce
- One teaspoon red pepper flakes
- One teaspoon sugar Pinch of salt

DIRECTIONS

Combine the lime juice, fish sauce, red pepper flakes, sugar, and salt in a small bowl and set aside. Leftover fish sauce? Add just a dash to tomato or marinara sauce to give it more depth of flavor and a faint, pleasant, salty note.

52. Crisscrossed Crab Cakes

IRON: Belgian or standard | TIME: 20 minutes | YIELD: Makes four crab cakes

INGREDIENTS

- One large egg,
- with a pinch of salt
- Pinch of cayenne pepper or curry powder

DIRECTIONS

1. Preheat the waffle iron on high. Preheat the oven on its lowest setting.

2. In a small bowl, mix the egg, cayenne pepper, and black pepper. Set aside.

3. In a medium-size bowl, gently combine the crab, bread crumbs, bell pepper, and chopped shallot. Add the egg mixture, stirring gently to incorporate it evenly into the dry ingredients.

4. Coat both sides of the waffle iron grid with nonstick spray. With a measuring cup, scoop out. 1/2 cup of the mixture and place it in the waffle iron. Close the lid and cook until the bread crumbs are golden brown and no liquid remains about 3 minutes.

5. Remove the crab cake from the waffle iron, spritz it with a lemon slice, and use the extra slices as garnish.

6. Repeat Steps 4 and 5 to make the remaining three crab cakes. Keep the finished crab cakes warm in the oven.Dollop a tablespoon of the Sriracha Mayonnaise on each crab cake, and serve.

53.Waffled Soft-Shell Crab

IRON: Belgian or standard | TIME: 15 minutes | YIELD: Serves 2

INGREDIENTS

- ½ cup all-purpose flour
- One teaspoon seafood seasoning mix, such as Old Bay
- Two soft-shell crabs
- Two tablespoons unsalted butter, melted.

DIRECTIONS

1. Preheat the waffle iron on high.

2. In a shallow bowl or deep dish, such as a pie plate, combine the flour and seasoning mix.

3. Pat a crab dry with paper towels. Dredge the crab in the flour, shake off the excess flour over the plate, and set aside the coated crab on a cutting board.

4. Using a silicone brush, coat both sides of the waffle iron grid with the melted butter.

5. Place the coated crab on the waffle iron, close the lid, and cook for 3 minutes. The coating should turn golden brown. If any raw flour remains on the crab, brush that spot with butter and continue to cook for another 30 seconds or so.

6. Repeat Steps 3 through 5 with the remaining crab.

54. Bibimbaffle (Waffled Bibimbap)

IRON: Belgian or standard | TIME: 20 minutes | YIELD: Serves 2

INGREDIENTS

- One tablespoon pure sesame oil
- 2 cups cooked white rice
- ½cup vegetable banchan, drained
- Two large eggs
- Salt and freshly ground black pepper, to taste
- Gochujang (hot pepper paste), to taste
- ½ cup kimchee
- Soy sauce, for drizzling (optional)

DIRECTIONS

1. Preheat the waffle iron on medium and use a silicone brush to coat both sides of the grid with sesame oil.

2. Place 1/2 cup rice on the waffle iron and distribute it evenly. Sprinkle about half of the vegetables on the rice, and then cover with another 1/2 cup rice, evenly distributed.

3. Close the lid of the waffle iron and cook until the rice is crispy about 8 minutes. Repeat Step 2 with the remaining rice and veggies, using another coat of sesame oil if needed.

4. While the rice and vegetables are cooking, fry the egg. Place a nonstick pan over high heat and fry a sunny egg side up until it's crispy on the bottom and soft on top, about 1 minute. Remove the egg from the pan and season it with salt and pepper. Repeat with the second egg.

5. Assemble your plate with the crispy waffled rice on the bottom, the egg on top, a spoonful or more of hot pepper paste as A garnish and a generous spoonful of kimchee on the side. Season with a splash or two of soy sauce and

serve.

55. Waffled Tamale Pie

IRON: Belgian or standard (Belgian will TIME: 30 minutes YIELD: Serves four yield a better topping-to-crust ratio)

INGREDIENTS

Topping:

- One tablespoon extra-virgin olive oil
- One large onion, finely chopped
- 1 pound ground turkey or beef
- One jalapeño pepper, minced (remove seeds for less heat)
- One teaspoon ground cumin

- One can (15 ounces) of crushed tomatoes.
- Salt and freshly ground black pepper, to taste

Crust:
- 1½ cups masa harina
- One teaspoon salt
- One teaspoon baking powder
- ¼teaspoon freshly ground black pepper
- 1 cup milk
- Four tablespoons (½ stick) unsalted butter, melted.
- One large egg, beaten Nonstick cooking spray
- 1 cup shredded sharp Cheddar cheese

DIRECTIONS

1. Make the topping: Place the olive oil in a large frying pan and add the onion. Sauté over medium heat until the onion just begins to brown, about 5 minutes. Remove the onion and set it aside on a plate.

2. Crumble the meat into the same skillet, browning it until no traces of pink remain, about 5 minutes. Pour off the excess fat and add the sautéed onion, jalapeño, cumin, and tomatoes to the pan until just heated through

about 1 minute. Taste and add salt and pepper. Let the mixture simmer over low heat while making the crust.

3. Preheat the waffle iron on medium.

4. Make the crust: In a large bowl, combine the masa harina, salt, baking powder, and black pepper. In a medium-size bowl, whisk the milk and the melted butter until combined, then whisk in the egg.

5. 5 Add the wet ingredients to the dry ingredients and stir to combine. The batter will be very thick.

6. Coat both sides of the waffle iron grid with nonstick spray. Divide the dough into four equal portions, about 1/2 cup each. Take a portion of the dough and pat it into a disk about the size of one section of the waffle iron. Repeat with the remaining three portions of dough.

7. Place the disks on the waffle iron, covering the waffle iron grid completely. Close the lid and cook until mostly set but not quite golden brown, about 3 minutes.

8. Open the waffle iron, spoon an even layer of the topping roughly 1/2 inch thick across the crust,

and close the waffle iron for 1 minute. Open the waffle iron once more, top with the cheese, and close the waffle iron for 20 seconds to melt the cheese. Remove the tamale pies from the waffle iron and serve.

56.Waffled Mexican Migas

IRON: Belgian or standard | TIME: 15 minutes | YIELD: Serves 2

INGREDIENTS

- Four large eggs
- One small tomato, diced (about ½ cup)
- ½ cup diced onion
- ½ cup shredded Cheddar or Monterey Jack cheese
- One small jalapeño pepper, seeded and minced
- Two soft corn tortillas, cut or torn into about ½-inch pieces
- ¼ teaspoon salt
- ¼ teaspoon freshly ground
- black pepper

- Nonstick cooking spray

DIRECTIONS

1. Preheat the waffle iron on medium.
2. In a medium-size bowl, beat the eggs. Add the rest of the ingredients except the cooking spray and stir vigorously to combine.
3. Coat both sides of the waffle iron grid with nonstick spray. Ladle some of the mixtures onto each section of the waffle iron. Some ingredients may settle to the bottom of the bowl, so make sure you reach the bottom of the bowl to get a good mixture.
4. Close the lid and cook until the eggs are no longer runny, 2 minutes.
5. Remove the gas from the waffle iron with an offset spatula or a pair of heat-resistant silicone spatulas and serve.

57.Waffled Chicken Fingers

IRON: Belgian or standard | TIME: 30 minutes | YIELD: Serves 4

INGREDIENTS

- ¾ cup all-purpose flour two large eggs
- Hot sauce, such as Tabasco, to taste
- 1½ cups plain bread crumbs
- ¼ cup grated Parmesan cheese
- Finely grated zest of 1 lemon one teaspoon salt
- One teaspoon freshly ground black pepper
- 1½ pounds boneless, skinless chicken cutlet
- Nonstick cooking spray
- Dipping sauces (recipes follow)

DIRECTIONS

1. Preheat the waffle iron on medium.

2. Place the flour in a shallow bowl or deep plate. In a second shallow bowl or deep plate, beat the eggs with a few drops of hot sauce.

3. In a third shallow bowl or deep plate combine the bread crumbs, Parmesan, and lemon zest. Add 1/2 teaspoon of the salt and 1/2 teaspoon of the pepper and stir to combine.

4. Put a single layer of the chicken in a zip-top bag, set it on a flat surface, and press down on the chicken with a cutting board, rolling pin, or heavy frying pan. Pound the chicken to a thickness of about 1/4 inch. Remove the chicken from the bag and cut it into strips about an inch wide. Repeat with the remaining chicken.

5. Season the chicken strips with the remaining 1/2 teaspoon each of the salt and pepper. Working in batches, dredge it in the flour, shaking off any excess. Transfer it to the bowl with the egg and turn the chicken to coat.

6. Allow the excess egg mixture to drip back into the bowl, and then coat the chicken with the bread crumb mixture, pressing the mixture, so

it sticks.

7. Coat both sides of the waffle iron grid with nonstick spray. Place the chicken in the waffle iron, close the lid, and cook until golden brown and cooked through, 4 minutes.

8. Remove the chicken from the waffle iron and serve with sauces of your choice.

58. Sweet-and-Sour Waffled Shrimp Wontons

IRON: Belgian or standard | TIME: 45 minutes | YIELD: Makes 16 wontons

INGREDIENTS

- 8 ounces cooked and chilled shrimp (31–40 count or 41–50 count), peeled, tails removed
- One large egg white, lightly beaten
- ¼ cup finely chopped scallion, both green and white parts
- One clove garlic, minced
- Two teaspoons light brown sugar
- Two teaspoons distilled white vinegar
- ½ teaspoon grated or minced fresh ginger

- ¾ teaspoon salt
- ½teaspoon freshly ground black pepper
- One package wonton wrappers (at least 32 wrappers), about 3½ inches per side
- Nonstick cooking spray
- Ginger-Sesame Dipping Sauce (recipe follows)

DIRECTIONS

1. Finely chop the shrimp so that they end up as almost a paste. If you want to use a food processor, half dozen quick pulses should accomplish this. Place the chopped shrimp in a medium-sized bowl.
2. Add the egg white, scallion, garlic, sugar, vinegar, ginger, salt, and pepper to the shrimp, stir to mix thoroughly, and set aside.
3. Preheat the waffle iron on high. Preheat the oven on its lowest setting.
4. To form the dumplings, remove a wonton wrapper from the package. Using a pastry brush or a clean finger, wet all. Four edges of the wrapper. Place a scant tablespoon of the shrimp mixture in the center and top with another wonton wrapper. Press along the edges

to seal. The water should act as glue. If you find a spot that's not sticking, add a bit more water. Set aside the finished wonton, cover with a damp towel, and shape the rest.

5. Coat both sides of the waffle iron grid with nonstick spray. Set as many wontons on the waffle iron as will comfortably fit and close the lid. Cook for 2 minutes before checking. The wonton wrapper should lose its translucency, and the waffle marks should be deep golden brown. This may take up to 4 minutes. Remove the cooked wontons and keep them warm in the oven while the others cook.

6. Serve the wontons with the Ginger-Sesame Dipping Sauce.

59. Crispy Sesame Waffled Kale

IRON: Belgian or standard | TIME: 30 minutes | YIELD: Serves 2

INGREDIENTS

- One bunch kale, washed and thoroughly dried, thick stems removed.
- Two teaspoons sesame oil blend or neutral-flavored oil, such as canola or grapeseed, mixed with a few drops of pure sesame oil
- Kosher salt, to taste

DIRECTIONS

1. Preheat the waffle iron on Medium heat.

2. In a large bowl, toss the kale with the oil to coat.

3. Place as much of the kale as will fit in the waffle iron, covering the grid. Some overlap is fine, so don't worry too much about placing it in a single layer. The kale will cook down considerably, so it need not all lie flat; the pressure of the waffle iron lid.

4. Close the waffle iron lid for 30 seconds, then open and redistribute the kale for a more even layer. Close the lid again. After 8 minutes, check on the kale. Some pieces may finish before others. Remove those pieces and place them on a plate. It may take up to 15 minutes for the kale to become crispy and chiplike.

5. Repeat Steps 3 and 4 with the remaining kale.

6. Sprinkle with salt and serve.

60. Caprese Salad with Waffled Eggplant

IRON: Belgian or standard TIME: 40 minutes, including 30 minutes for salting eggplant YIELD: Serves 2

INGREDIENTS

- One small eggplant, cut into round slices about ½ inch thick.
- Kosher salt orcoarse sea salt and freshly ground black pepper, to taste
- Two medium-size ripe tomatoes
- 4 ounces fresh mozzarella
- ¼ cup extra-virgin olive oil, plus more for drizzling

- One large bunch of basil, washed and dried, stems removed.

DIRECTIONS

1. Place the eggplant slices on a layer of paper towels and generously sprinkle both sides of the slices with salt. Allow the eggplant to sit for 30 minutes.
2. Meanwhile, slice the tomatoes into rounds. Do the same with the mozzarella.
3. Preheat the waffle iron on high.
4. Rinse the eggplant slices in cold water to wash off the salt. Pat the slices dry. Brush both sides of each eggplant slice with olive oil.
5. Place the eggplant in the waffle iron, close the lid, and cook until the eggplant is soft and cooked through 4 minutes.
6. Remove the eggplant from the waffle iron and set it on a serving plate, layering it with slices of tomatoes and cheese. Scatter the basil leaves atop the salad. Drizzle with olive oil and sprinkle with salt and freshly ground pepper.

61. Waffletons (Waffled Croutons)

IRON: Belgian or standard TIME: 30 minutes YIELD: 8 cups; serves 8

INGREDIENTS

- Three slices thick bread,
- or 2 Belgian-style waffles, cut into cubes
- Two cloves garlic
- ½ cup extra-virgin olive oil
- One tablespoon grated Parmesan cheese
- Pinch of salt
- ¼ teaspoon freshly ground
- black pepper

DIRECTIONS

1. If you're using bread, preheat the waffle iron on medium. If you're using waffles, preheat the oven to 450°F.

2. Crush the garlic cloves with the flat side of a knife blade. Place the garlic and the cubed. Read or waffles in a medium-size bowl with the oil, cheese, Salt and pepper. Stir to combine. Allow everything to soak for 5 minutes, toss and then allow to soak another 5 minutes.

3. IF YOU'RE USING BREAD: Place the soaked bread cubes in the preheated waffle iron, close the lid, and cook for 5 minutes Before checking on them. The waffled croutons are done when they are mostly golden brown, though the waffle indentations It may be a darker brown.

4. Serve the croutons with your favorite salad or sprinkle them on top of tomato soup.

62.Waffled Pajeon (Korean Scallion Pancake)

IRON: Belgian or standard | TIME: 10 minutes | YIELD: Serves 4

 INGREDIENTS

- 1 cup all-purpose flour
- 1½ teaspoons granulated sugar
- One teaspoon salt
- 1 cup water
- Ten scallions washed and dried
- Nonstick cooking spray
- Sesame-Soy Dipping Sauce (recipe follows)

DIRECTIONS

1. Preheat the waffle iron.

2. In a medium-size bowl, medium. Combine the flour, sugar, and Salt. Add the water and whisk just until combined.

3. Trim away the white bottoms of the scallions. (See the headnote for what to do with the white parts.) Trim the tops of the scallions if they are ragged and sad. Cut the stems so that they are roughly the length of one section of your waffle iron.

4. Coat both sides of the waffle iron grid with nonstick spray. Arrange a small handful of scallions on the waffle iron. For the best-looking pajeon, set the scallions in the "valleys" of the waffle iron and arrange them in a crisscross pattern. Pour about 1⁄4 cup of batter on top and close the waffle iron.

5. Cook until the batter has set and the scallions have cooked through 4 minutes. You can poke one of the scallions with the Tip of a sharp knife to see if it has cooked.

6. Remove the pajeon from the waffle iron and repeat Steps 4 and 5 with the remaining

scallions and batter.

7. Serve with the Sesame-Soy.

63.Halloumi (Waffled Haloumi Cheese) and Watermelon

IRON: Belgian or standard | TIME: 15 minutes | YIELD: Serves 4

INGREDIENTS

- 8 ounces halloumi, cut into eight slices
- Small seedless watermelon
- Extra-virgin olive oil for drizzling
- Salt and freshly ground black pepper, to taste

DIRECTIONS

1. Preheat the waffle iron on medium.

2. Slice the watermelon into eight wedges about 1⁄2 inch thick— big enough to accommodate a piece of waffled cheese stacked atop them. Trim off the rind if you'd like, or leave it on to add a splash of color to the dish. Set the watermelon wedges aside.

3. Place the cheese slices on the waffle iron and close the lid.

4. Cook for 2 minutes before checking. The cheese is ready when it has waffle marks and turns golden brown in most spots.

5. To serve, stack a piece of waffled cheese atop each watermelon wedge and drizzle with olive oil. Sprinkle with salt and pepper to taste.

64.Cheesy Waffled Arancini

IRON: Belgian or standard | TIME: 30 minutes | YIELD: Makes eight arancini; serves 4

INGREDIENTS

- 2 cups cooked short-grain white rice such as Arborio, prepared according to package directions and cooled
- ½ cup grated Parmesan cheese
- ¼ teaspoon salt
- ¼ teaspoon freshly ground black pepper
- Three large eggs
- 2 ounces fresh mozzarella, cut into eight chunks
- 1 cup seasoned bread crumbs
- Nonstick cooking spray

- 1 cup marinara sauce

DIRECTIONS

1. Preheat the waffle iron on medium. Preheat the oven on its lowest setting.
2. In a medium-size bowl, combine the rice, Parmesan, salt, pepper, and 1 of the eggs, and stir to thoroughly blend.
3. With wet hands, form each rice ball by taking a small portion of the mixture, squeezing it firmly into a ball, and stuffing a chunk of mozzarella inside the ball. The cheese should be completely encased in the rice.
4. Repeat this process to form 8 arancini balls and set them aside.
5. Whisk together the remaining two eggs in a small bowl. Set the bread crumbs in a shallow bowl or deep dish, such as a pie pan. Dip each of the arancini in the egg mixture and then in the bread crumbs, shaking off any excess. Handle the arancini delicately. (Don't worry too much, though—if one falls apart, just press it back together.)

6. Coat both sides of the waffle iron grid with nonstick spray. Place a ball of arancini in each section of the waffle iron, close the lid, and cool until the arancini hold together as a cohesive unit, 4 minutes.

7. While the arancini are cooking, heat the marinara sauce in the microwave for 45 seconds or in a small saucepan on the stovetop over low heat.

8. Remove the arancini from the waffle iron and repeat Steps 5 and 6 with the remaining arancini. Keep the finished arancini warm in the oven.

9. Serve arancini with warm marinara sauce.

65. Waffled Tostones

IRON: Belgian or standard (with a Belgian-style iron, tostones will have to be arranged on the grid for the maximum number of waffle marks) TIME: 30 minutes YIELD: Serves 4

INGREDIENTS

- 2 quarts of neutral-flavored oil, such as canola, for frying
- Two yellow plantains
- (a little bit of green is fine) Salt, to taste
- Garlic Dipping Sauce

DIRECTIONS

1. Pour the oil into a large pot or Dutch oven, taking care to leave plenty of room at the top of the pot. The oil must not come up more than halfway, or it could bubble over when the plantains are added.

2. Bring the oil to 350°F on an instant-read thermometer over medium heat.

3. While the oil heats, peel the plantains. Slice off each end and then cut three slits lengthwise along the plantain. Pry the skin off with your fingers. Cut each plantain into slices about 1/4 inch thick.

4. Preheat the waffle iron on Medium. Warm a platter in the oven on its lowest setting.

5. When the oil reaches about 350°F, a cube of bread dropped into the oil will turn light brown in 60 seconds. Fry the plantain slices at this temperature for 1 minute.

6. After a minute, check a Plantain slice to see if it's done. It should be a light golden color and cooked on the outside. The

7. Greener the plantain is, the longer it will take to fry—up to about 3 minutes.

8. With a slotted spoon, remove the fried plantains from the oil and drain on a plate lined with paper towels. A little oil clinging. To them is fine—in fact, it will help when they go into the waffle iron.

9. Place as many fried plantains as will fit in a single layer on the waffle iron, leaving a bit of room for them to expand.

10. Press the cover of the waffle iron down to smash the plantains flat. Careful: The lid may be hot.

11. Cook until the plantains are a deep golden brown and are soft throughout, 2 minutes.

12. Remove the plantains from the waffle iron. Repeat Steps 8 through 10 with the remaining plantains.

13. Place finished plantains on a warm platter and sprinkle with salt. Serve with the Garlic Dipping Sauce.

66.Waffled Fries

IRON: Belgian or standard | TIME: 10 minutes | YIELD: Serves 4

INGREDIENTS

- Nonstick cooking spray
- Four tablespoons (½ stick) unsalted butter, melted
- 1 cup water
- ½ teaspoon salt
- 2 cups instant potato flakes
- Ketchup or mayonnaise for serving

DIRECTIONS

1. Preheat the waffle iron on high. Coat both sides of the waffle iron grid with nonstick spray.

2. Combine the melted butter, water, and salt in a bowl. Add the potato flakes and stir the mixture thoroughly. Allow it to sit while the waffle iron comes to the desired temperature. The mixture will be quite thick.

3. For each waffled fry, put about a tablespoon of potato mixture in the waffle iron. Fit as much of the potato mixture as you can on the waffle iron grid, close the lid, and cook until deep golden brown, 3 minutes. Remove the fries and repeat, spraying the waffle iron grid again if necessary, until you have used up all of the potato mixtures.

4. Serve the fries with ketchup or mayonnaise.

67. S'moreffles (Waffled S'mores)

IRON: Belgian or standard TIME: 30 minutes
YIELD: Serves 4
INGREDIENTS

- Nonstick cooking spray
- ½cup white whole wheat flour
- ½ cup all-purpose flour
- ¼ cup firmly packed dark brown sugar
- ½ teaspoon baking soda ¼ teaspoon salt
- Pinch of ground cinnamon
- Four tablespoons (½ stick) unsalted butter, melted.
- Two tablespoons milk

- ¼ cup honey
- One tablespoon pure vanilla extract
- ¾cup semisweet chocolate chips
- ¾ cup mini marshmallows

DIRECTIONS

1. Preheat the waffle iron on medium. Coat both sides of the waffle iron grid with nonstick spray.
2. In a mixing bowl, combine the flours, brown sugar, baking soda, salt, and cinnamon. In a separate bowl, whisk together the melted butter, milk, honey, and vanilla.
3. Add the wet ingredients to the flour mixture and stir until a dough forms.
4. Let the mixture stand for 5 minutes. It will be much thicker than ordinary waffle batter but not as thick as bread dough.
5. Measure out about 1/4 cup of batter and place it on one section of the waffle iron. Repeat with another 1/4 cup of batter to give you a top and a bottom for your s'moreffle sandwich.
6. Close the lid and cook until the waffled graham crackers are still slightly soft but cooked throughout 3 minutes.

7. Carefully remove the waffled graham crackers from the waffle iron. They will be quite soft, so use care to keep them intact. Allow them to cool slightly. Repeat Steps 5 to 7 with the rest of the batter.

68.Waffle Croque

IRON: Belgian or standard TIME: 5 hours YIELD: Serves up to 6

INGREDIENTS

- One-piece crescent dough or Brioche Dough
- 3 tablespoons Béchamel Sauce
- Two slices of the Black Forest ham
- ¼ cup shredded Gruyère cheese
- One large egg

DIRECTIONS

Preheat the waffle iron on medium.

IF YOU'RE USING CRESCENT DOUGH:

The dough will likely come out of the tube in a wedge shape, but it can be assembled into a square. Cut the wedge of dough in half to make two triangles. Shape the triangles into a yard 4 to 5 inches on each side and press the edges together gently. Using a silicone brush, coat both sides of one section of the waffle iron with the melted butter, place the dough on that section of the waffle iron, close the lid, and cook the dough is golden brown for about 3 minutes. Remove the dough from the waffle iron and transfer it to a cutting board or plate.

IF YOU'RE USING BRIOCHE DOUGH:

Using a silicone brush, coat both sides of one section of the waffle iron with the melted butter and cook the dough on one area of the waffle iron with the lid closed until the dough is golden brown, about 4 minutes. Remove the dough from the waffle iron and transfer it to a cutting board or plate.

3 Pour the Béchamel Sauce onto the waffled dough. (The sauce will mostly pool in the divots.) Then layer

the ham on top. Sprinkle the shredded cheese on top. Place the assembled stack in the waffle iron and close the lid for 10 seconds to melt the cheese and marry the layers. Remove the stack from the waffle iron.

Crack an egg into a small cup or ramekin. This will give you control over how the egg lands on the waffle iron. Brush the remaining melted butter on the lower grid of one section of the waffle iron and pour the egg onto that section. Cook, without closing the lid, until the white.

69.Waffled Sweet Potato Gnocchi

IRON: Standard preferred | TIME: 2 hours | YIELD: Serves 4 (makes about 60 gnocchi)

INGREDIENTS

- One large baking potato (such as russet) and one large sweet potato (about 1½ pounds total)
- 1¼ cups all-purpose flour, plus more for flouring the work surface
- ½ cup grated Parmesan cheese
- One teaspoon salt
- ½ teaspoon freshly ground black pepper
- Dash of grated nutmeg (optional)

- One large egg, beaten.
- Nonstick cooking spray or melted butter
- Pesto or Waffled Sage

DIRECTIONS

1. Preheat the oven to 350°F.

2. Bake the potatoes until easily pierced with a fork, about an hour. Let the potatoes cool slightly, and then peel them. (They may be just shy of the texture you'd want in a baked potato, but keep in mind they're being cooked again later.) Pass the potatoes through a food mill or a ricer or grate them over the large holes of a box grater and into a large bowl.

3. Add the 1 1/4 cups flour to the potatoes and use your hands to mix them, breaking up any lumps of potato along the way. Sprinkle the cheese, salt, pepper, and nutmeg over the dough and knead lightly to distribute evenly.

4. Once the flour and potatoes are combined, make a well in the bowl's center and add the beaten egg. Using your fingers, work the egg through the dough. Until it starts to come together, it will be slightly sticky.

5. On a lightly floured surface, gently knead the dough a few times to bring it together. It should be moist but not wet and sticky. If it's too sticky, add one tablespoon flour at a time, up to 1/4 cup. Roll the dough into a log and cut it into four pieces.

6. Roll each piece into a rope about the diameter of your thumb and then use a sharp knife to cut into 1-inch segments.

7. Preheat the waffle iron on medium. Coat both sides of the waffle iron grid with nonstick spray, or butter the grids using a silicone pastry brush. Turn down the oven to its lowest setting and set aside a baking sheet to keep the finished gnocchi warm and serve!

70. Pressed Potato and Cheese Pierogi

IRON: Standard preferred | TIME: 2 hours | YIELD: Serves 4 (makes about 60 gnocchi)

INGREDIENTS

- One large baking potato (such as russet) and one large sweet potato (about 1½ pounds total)
- 1¼ cups all-purpose flour, plus more for flouring the work surface
- ½ cup grated Parmesan cheese
- One teaspoon salt
- ½ teaspoon freshly ground black pepper
- Dash of grated nutmeg (optional)
- One large egg, beaten.

- Nonstick cooking spray or melted butter
- Pesto or Waffled Sage and Butter Sauce

DIRECTIONS

1. Preheat the oven to 350°F.

2. Bake the potatoes until easily pierced with a fork, about an hour. Let the potatoes cool slightly, and then peel them. (They may be just shy of the texture you'd want in a baked potato, but keep in mind they're being cooked again later.) Pass the potatoes through a food mill or a ricer or grate them over the large holes of a box grater and into a large bowl.

3. Add the 1 1/4 cups flour to the potatoes and use your hands to mix them, breaking up any lumps of potato along the way. Sprinkle the cheese, salt, pepper, and nutmeg over the dough and knead lightly to distribute evenly.

4. Once the flour and potatoes are combined, make a well in the bowl's center and add the beaten egg. Using your fingers, work the egg through the dough. Until it starts to come together, it will be slightly sticky.

5. On a lightly floured surface, gently knead the dough a few times to bring it together. It should be moist but not wet and sticky. If it's too sticky, add one tablespoon flour at a time, up to 1/4 cup. Roll the dough into a log and cut it into four pieces.

6. Roll each piece into a rope about the diameter of your thumb and then use a sharp knife to cut into 1-inch segments.

7. Preheat the waffle iron on medium. Coat both sides of the waffle iron grid with nonstick spray, or butter the grids using a silicone pastry brush. Turn down the oven to its lowest setting and set aside a baking sheet to keep the finished gnocchi warm and serve!

71.Chicken Parmesan with Waffled Vegetables

IRON: Belgian or standard | TIME: 30 minutes | YIELD: Serves 4

INGREDIENTS

- ¾ cup all-purpose flour two large eggs
- Hot sauce, such as Tabasco, to taste
- 1½ cups plain bread crumbs
- ¼cup grated Parmesan cheese
- Finely grated zest of 1 lemon one teaspoon salt
- One teaspoon freshly ground black pepper
- Four boneless, skinless chicken cutlets (1½ pounds total)
- Nonstick cooking spray

- ½ cup grated mozzarella cheese
- Waffled Vegetables (recipe follows)
- Fresh whole basil leaves (optional)

DIRECTIONS

1. Preheat the waffle iron on medium.
2. Place the flour in a shallow bowl or deep plate. In a second shallow bowl or deep plate, beat the eggs with a few hot sauce drops.
3. In a third shallow bowl or deep plate combine the bread crumbs, Parmesan, and lemon zest. Add 1⁄2 teaspoon of the salt and 1⁄2 teaspoon of the pepper.
4. Bring the marinara sauce to a simmer in a small saucepan over medium-low heat.
5. Put a single layer of the chicken in a zip-top bag, set it on a flat surface, and press down on the chicken with a cutting board, rolling pin, or heavy frying pan until the chicken is about 1⁄4 inch thick.
6. Remove the chicken from the bag, place it on a clean cutting board, and sprinkle the remaining 1⁄2 teaspoon of each salt and pepper over it.

7. Repeat Steps 5 and 6 with the remaining chicken.

8. Dredge a chicken cutlet in the flour, shaking off any excess. Transfer it to the bowl with the egg and turn the chicken to coat. Allow the excess egg mixture to drip back into the bowl, and then coat the chicken with the bread crumb mixture, pressing the mixture to the chicken, so it sticks. Set it aside on a platter and repeat with the remaining chicken.

9. Coat both sides of the waffle iron grid with nonstick spray. Place the chicken in the waffle iron, close the lid, and cook until golden brown and cooked through, 4 minutes.

10. Top the chicken with the grated mozzarella and close the lid for 20 seconds to allow the cheese to melt. Remove the chicken from the waffle iron.

11. Ladle about 1/2 cup marinara sauce per portion onto a plate and then place the chicken on top of the sauce. Drizzle with

12. A little more sauce, add the waffled vegetables to the plate and garnish everything with the basil.

72.Fawaffle (Waffled Falafel) and Hummus

IRON: Belgian or standard TIME: 20 minutes, plus overnight YIELD: Serves four soaking for chickpeas

INGREDIENTS

- 1 cup dried chickpeas, picked over and soaked in water overnight in the refrigerator
- ½ small onion, roughly chopped
- Three cloves garlic
- ¼cup chopped fresh flat-leaf parsley
- Two tablespoons extra-virgin olive oil
- Two tablespoons all-purpose flour

- One teaspoon salt
- One teaspoon ground cumin
- ½ teaspoon ground coriander
- ¼ teaspoon baking powder
- ¼ teaspoon freshly ground
- black pepper
- ¼ teaspoon cayenne pepper Nonstick cooking spray
- Perfectly Smooth Hummus (recipe follows)
- Four pockets pita bread (optional)

DIRECTIONS

1. Preheat the waffle iron on medium. Preheat the oven on its lowest setting.
2. Drain the soaked chickpeas and place them with the onion and garlic in a food processor. Pulse until blended but not pureed.
3. Add the parsley, olive oil, flour, salt, cumin, coriander, baking powder, black pepper, cayenne pepper, and pulse until mostly smooth.
4. Coat both sides of the waffle iron grid with nonstick spray. For each waffle, place about 1/4 cup of batter in the waffle iron, leaving a bit of

space between scoops for each to expand.

5. Close the lid of the waffle iron and cook for 5 minutes before checking. Remove the waffles when they are cooked through and evenly browned.

6. Repeat Steps 4 and 5 with the remaining batter.

7. Keep finished waffles warm in the oven. Serve them with hummus and pita bread.

Conclusion

Chaffing is growing. For a long while, after I stopped blogging and while I was working on this book, I wasn't sure what to expect. Would waffling wane? I needn't have worried. Waffling did not stop. It spread. And yet, there's still more work to be done. Long maligned as single-purpose appliances, waffle irons have a reputation to overcome and baggage to shed. Counter space is tight, you say? I hear you. But that is most typically a thing said by people who don't use their waffle irons because, yes, counter space is too tight for things you don't use. Can't afford to buy a waffle iron, you say? Fair enough. Here's a thought: You may well know people who have one but do not use it. Quick! Convince them to give it to you before they find this book. (If that doesn't work, check yard sales, online auctions, for-sale listings, and thrift stores. Or hint a lot around the holidays or your birthday.) We have a lot of waffling to do. I'm almost done here. Let me leave you with this:

These pages are my answers to the question "Will it chaffle?" But my answers are just the beginning. By the end of this book, you will have the tools you need to continue experimenting and building your recipes. Muster your sense of culinary daring. We're going to see what the waffle iron can do.

CPSIA information can be obtained
at www.ICGtesting.com
Printed in the USA
BVHW090428300421
606133BV00004B/288